Coffins & Confetti

A CELEBRANT'S MEMOIR
OF LIFE, LOSS & LOVE

by Ruth Graham

Imprint: Independently Published

Design by Euan Monaghan
Cover illustration by Eva Polakovičová

ISBN 979-8-3983241-9-8

BOOKS BY RUTH GRAHAM

Coffins & Confetti (A Celebrant's Memoir Of Life, Loss & Love)
A Thousand Goodbyes (The Surprising Life Of A Funeral Celebrant)

Follow the author on Instagram @CelebrantRuthG

THANKS

Thank you to everyone who enjoyed the first book and encouraged me to write a second.

Thank you also to my editors and proof-readers on this project (Liz Morrell, Maxine Wakefield and Fiona Bennett-Heritage) as it changed from memoir, to autobiography, romantic fiction and back to a much-improved memoir again.

Thank you to Russ for allowing our private moments to be laid bare upon the page; and to my fellow celebrants for sharing your stories so generously.

This book is dedicated to the memory of Tim Maddocks.
A kinder, funnier man would be hard to find.

CHAPTERS

INTRODUCTION

Coffins & Confetti is a celebration of people and life. A sharing of my learnings from the extraordinary odyssey I've been on since discovering this wonderful work.

The stories are not told in chronological order but rather, presented in a way that helps with their flow and impact. I hope they entertain but above all that they encourage everyone to live in a way that's authentic and right for them whilst remembering we are all connected and part of one greater humanity. My final message is also to never give up on your dreams or the search for love. Enjoy!

CHAPTER 1: WHO ARE YOU?

'Celebrant': The dictionary definition will tell you this is a person who officiates at ceremonies.

After 8 years on the emotional frontline conducting 1,551 funerals; 137 weddings; 5 interments of ashes; 18 baby namings; 3 family blending ceremonies; 1 divorce healing service and 10 memorials of life, here's my thoughts:

'Celebrant':

A frequently knackered person.

Someone recognisable by their metaphorical balls of steel, very thick skin and their uncanny ability to cry inside without showing a tear. Part writer, public speaker, counsellor, secretary, journalist and event planner.

I'd also put tactician and crisis negotiator in there somewhere too, having dealt with warring families revealing the most dreadful secrets to each other at the twelfth hour, as well as people fainting during funerals, defecating dogs at romantic woodland weddings and a bride that was two hours late. Thinking on my feet, we ended up having a sing-song and playing musical chairs until she arrived!

It's not everyone who would choose this career, but the variety of people who do, and the reasons we do are fairly mind-boggling.

Casting my mind around my colleagues there's a varied roster of celebrants who once had very different lives as policemen or women, prison workers, florists, opticians, sales-people, entertainers, school teachers and journalists.

There's also a former vicar's wife, an ex-comedian (two if you include me); an ex-travel agent and a one-time chauffeur. Obviously dealing with death, sadness, irregular hours, difficult brides and absolutely no job security has wider appeal than one might think!

I say that with tongue in cheek of course; the actual appeal is doing a job of worth; something which provides a lasting, positive outcome for the majority of families. When people say they're "beyond grateful" and "will never forget you", it has the uncanny ability to quieten the imposter syndrome that lives inside most of us; wondering why we're here and what this random 'improv' show of life is all about.

As a childless person with no close family, that thought has regularly tapped on my ever-stiffening shoulders. The pointlessness of my existence during certain periods of life has been both mentally and physically debilitating at times.

I've sought to silence it in very many ways: for example, with disastrous relationships – I've got cheese in my fridge more mature than some of the idiots I've wasted myself on.

I've also changed jobs frequently, tried over-eating, under-eating and interestingly, I've also tried making myself indispensable: ("Yes, of course I'll lend you money/babysit/let you stay at mine for six months for free.")

I even took in a man off the streets for a while to try and rehabilitate him; all to feel needed, useful or even just noticed.

Visits to a National Health Service psychiatrist followed when I could stand it no more. He took copious notes during which I deflected, made jokes and cried. At the end of the consultation, it was obvious the over-stretched NHS was in no position to sort me out in one or two visits, so I left with a referral to see someone higher up the chain in six months' time.

Looking embarrassed at the length of the wait, the doctor also handed me an emergency 24-hour helpline number, 'In case you feel suicidal.' I called it twice and it was an answerphone …

Those days are long behind me now. Dealing with mother issues and ditching toxic friends was a key part of it, and the other part as I've said, is finding work with real meaning and purpose. I hypothesise that this is why most celebrants are middle aged and beyond.

Some have been spurred on by sitting through impersonal and badly written funeral services for friends or family and felt we could do better. Some prefer the freedom of being self-employed, whilst others have just sought a more fulfilling career.

Alongside this sits the reasoning that through our experiences, both good and bad, we've perhaps accrued more empathy and understanding, an ability to help people through the biggest days of their life, both happy and sad. I know I certainly did.

Doing this work also really helped validate my own existence; something I never experienced whilst temping/stuffing envelopes/selling sunbeds/teaching English/stand-up comedy or the other many careers I've endured.

However, one thing I did gain from these roles, as dull, menial or pointless as they seemed at the time, was an armoury of skills, all of which combined beautifully to prepare me for what I now do.

The typing pools improved my speed (imperative when writing services); the teaching improved my confidence, and the comedy gave me the skills to deal with any situation that might suddenly present itself. As for the writing – well, I think that was always there if I'm honest, but the opportunity to create something beautiful, to take the listener on a journey, is a real privilege.

In the case of funerals, it may be a journey to restore someone back to who they were at their best, for example, in the case of Alzheimer's where it's all too easy to just remember the struggles of the final years.

It doesn't do someone justice to remember them that way when the vast majority of their life will have been spent working, laughing, loving and raising a family so I do my very best to warm up the stories and get people smiling again as they hear them.

Alternatively, it may be a journey of forgiveness, when a spouse, parent or child has fallen short in some way. In this instance, I try and balance out the happy memories whilst pointing out that we are all fallible human beings. When it comes to remembering someone under these circumstances, the kindest thing we can do for ourselves is to love them for the things they did and the times they tried; and forgive them for their failings, as we'd hope others would do for us.

These are just a couple of approaches I use, depending on the circumstances, but my hope is always that by the end of the service, whatever the words or the emphasis; people have reached not only the point of acceptance that a life has ended, but also a place of peace.

By writing a personalised service, filled with anecdotes, stories, relevant readings, poems and music it really can help everyone leave, knowing their loved one has been thanked and honoured. Everything has been done properly, and that way there is no room for regret, guilt or lingering 'what ifs?' In turn, this allows a family to move on with the rest of their own lives in a more positive way.

Sometimes though, a family doesn't feel the need for a celebrant to help them reach that stage. They feel confident they're able to conduct their own personal service and we're most definitely not invited. This is exactly what I witnessed a few years ago when I got to the crem twenty minutes or so before my slot.

Pottering into the foyer, my usual routine is to greet the chapel attendant, grab a glass of water, check the music has been loaded onto the system in the correct order and then read through my notes. However, that went straight out the window when I saw and heard what was happening.

As the music to what I now know to be Torpedo Los! a Nazi march from the Third Reich blasted out, a large family group, (approximately twenty in total), paraded stiff-legged up to the coffin. Even the old lady with a Zimmer frame was doing her best!

After touching the coffin, they then stood back in a semi-formal line. Someone produced a Nazi flag and shouted "Seig Heil" followed by a group salute. It was like a pastiche of something from Monty Python, or perhaps the Springtime For Hitler scene in the play The Producers. I just couldn't take it in.

"What on earth's going on?" I half-gasped, half asked Kenny, the chapel attendant.

He did his usual 'I-don't-know-and-I-don't-care' shrug, the one he brings out for most occasions because he can't be arsed with anything. Kenny is just biding his time until retirement, which he'll gleefully, hand-rubbingly tell you (in the strongest of Birmingham accents) is, "Just twelve years away now!"

For anyone who cares to look, Kenny is usually found loping around the crem's chapel, emerging from the shadows at the last second to do his work, which as far as I can ascertain seems to consist solely of checking the name plate on the coffin against his official documentation.

He'll then say "Alright mate, go ahead" to whoever happens to be leading the service. (I heard on the grapevine once that Kenny actually used to say "Crack on", but I think someone had a word with him about being overly-casual.)

After performing this one duty, Kenny then melts into the background, phone already in hand to check the horse racing results even before he's reached the back office. This is where he brews his endless cups of tar-coloured tea that he gulps from his filthy Birmingham City mug – the one that has remained proudly un-washed for almost a decade, because he 'doesn't believe in that sort of thing.'

The epitome of an over-promiser and under-deliverer, if Kenny said he was going to lend you a spade, he'd turn up (three days late) with a mustard spoon.

If I ask for extra chairs for the service, he'll make as if he's going to the store cupboard but then he'll shrug mock-apologetically and tell me it's above his pay grade.

When a bird once got trapped inside the building, I asked Kenny to open one of the really high windows to give the poor thing a chance to escape. This would have required him to walk all of twenty steps to fetch a pole.

I watched indifference and stubbornness flash across his face as he considered the request, before settling on the decision to not bother. Instead, Kenny plumped for appeasement, telling me it would 'add some interest' for the mourners. He literally is about as useful as a wheelchair in a lighthouse.

This particular time, after the obligatory shoulder shrug, Kenny's answer to my question about what was happening was: "Well, the family have hired the room and are doing it themselves. I s'pose they can do what they like within reason. As long as they don't start a fight or burn the place down, what can I do?"

I was aghast. Was a Nazi-themed funeral 'within reason?' But then again this was family, and they were all plainly of the same mind-set; nobody in that room was offended.

Here was a group of people celebrating someone they loved in their own personal, meaningful way, although I had to admit it did pose a dilemma. Where would I draw my own line? What would I say if a family asked me to do something that I felt was personally offensive?

The funeral director (FD) Bryan agreed it was a dilemma. His company had been engaged solely to prepare the body and then deliver it to the crematorium. At the end of it his only duty then was to remove the charming Swastika flower arrangement and carry it out to the Garden of Rest. There it would sit until it was got at by the weather or hopefully sooner, by the resident rabbits.

"Now't so queer as folk though is there?" said Bryan, "but at least it keeps us in business."

He was referring to the very heavy push these days for direct cremations (marketed as 'Pure Cremations' in the UK). In these instances, there is no funeral service and no mourners; it's just an unattended cremation. This leaves people free to hold a memorial service afterwards to celebrate their loved one's life in their own way, at the venue and time of their choosing.

Just as an aside, both options, direct cremation and celebrating someone's life after the event, have always been available to people. It's nothing new but because it's not a profitable option (and because most people actually *do* want to attend a funeral) it's not generally mentioned when a family go to visit an FD.

I get that. As someone who has conducted beautiful, personal ceremonies in a variety of settings from woodland glades to someone's own garden at home, (as well as the standard more traditional venues, of course), I can see how much people need the tradition of gathering together in love and loss. This public witnessing is a huge part of the ritual, so the rise of Pure Cremations is interesting.

I can only conclude their success must be to do with people's finances, which is very sad if that is the case. When a person has been loved and cherished by friends and families a direct cremation seems a rather impersonal way to end their time on this earth.

The very essence of a celebrant-led service is to help others celebrate a life, and the witnessing of this is a key part of it for the majority of families.

We saw this time and again during the Covid pandemic, when crematoriums were forced to reduce their congregations to as few as six mourners.

Too many families were heartbroken at not being able to spend those precious moments with others who felt the same. I've lost count of the times people said things like "It's such a shame, it would have been packed today."

One family felt this so deeply, that we were asked to tape A4-sized pictures of every missing mourner to the backs of the benches prior to the start of the service. The FD and I ran around frantically with our sticky tape, scissors and pictures, and ten minutes later the chapel was transformed.

We conducted that service to six living souls and 150 photographs. For obvious reasons that is one occasion I'll never forget.

CHAPTER 2: AND WHERE DO YOU DO IT?

With regards to funeral side of the work, I cover several crematoria around the city of Birmingham in the UK; a sprawling metropolis encompassing both the wealthiest and the most deprived areas in the country.

At its most authentic, Birmingham is pure Peaky Blinders territory, characterised by the few remaining cobbled streets and warehouses that nestle under the Victorian arches off Constitution Hill and St Paul's Square.

The sense of history is palpable; every time I walk around the area I wonder how many dodgy deals were finalised? Who traded in the shadows from behind the huge wooden doors, set into the ancient brick walls like the defences of a castle?

Things open out towards the centre of the city, which houses the majority of the Victorian and Edwardian architecture, typified by the gothic turrets of the Law Courts and the classical columns of the City Council House. And then around this, Birmingham defies any categorisation at all.

Just minutes apart, grand houses can give way to converted loft apartments, then council homes (project homes), student accommodation and then back to wealth.

It's a tangle of sprawling ring roads, the most famous of which is known as 'Spaghetti Junction'; then small side streets and backed up traffic going nowhere.

Glass tower blocks, seemingly springing up at the rate of one a week, sit next to tiny homes. And to boot, the canal system runs right through the centre of it all.

I love the place as it's my home-town, but Birmingham has long ceased to make any sense. I swear the job description for City Planner must have included the line: 'Colour-blind, glass and steel loving, crack-smoking visionaries required.'

The crems I work at also vary wildly. Mostly run by the local authority, the buildings are jaded, faded and in need of refurbishment. The curtains hold decades of cobwebs, the heating regularly breaks down and every one of them has the feel of somewhere that has given up. I often think that if I was saying goodbye to a loved one, would I really want it to be somewhere like that?

Happily, there are also a couple of private crems (owned by funeral chains as part of a larger business model). These definitely stand out for being cleaner, more efficient and, I hate to say it, for having more helpful and dedicated staff. There are no prizes for guessing which one Kenny works at (!), but regardless, I'll refer to all of these establishments generically as 'the crem' throughout the book.

Each one has national industry rules and standards to abide by, and then additionally some have their own set of peculiar rules and idiosyncrasies, depending on the management. Universally though, they all dislike anything out of the norm.

Requests turned down so far on my watch include a family who wanted to take a swig of beer from a pint glass at the end of the service (not allowed to 'Covid overhang', whatever that was); and the rather more amusing request to wave a puppet from behind the curtain as it closed.

That was from the family of a man who had been a cabaret ventriloquist on the working men's club circuit. They wanted his puppet character to say something rude and give a cheery wave as his finale.

Sadly, for health and safety reasons, they weren't allowed, but if it had been up to me I'd have said a big yes; partly because I'm a boundary-pusher, and partly because celebrants are usually facilitators by nature.

It's also what we're trained to do; to go the extra mile; to think differently and creatively to give people beautiful, memorable experiences. Whether it's a funeral or a wedding, it's all about making things personal if that's what the family wants.

This not standing near the curtain thing was a mystery to me. Like I said, I'd have been all for it: 'Go ahead. Yes – let's make this fun and personal. Let the mourners leave feeling uplifted, with a smile on their faces.' But it wasn't to be.

I'm not sure what havoc the crem assistant imagined a puppet and a curtain could wreak? Perhaps they thought the puppeteer would trip and bring it down? Or more likely, the worry may have been they'd inhale the decades of dust lingering in the folds of fabric, years later going on to sue the council for some terrible newly-named disease? ('I'm sorry to tell you sir it's confirmed: you've got 'Pelmet Lung'.)

Perhaps the real reason was that some of the mystery of the occasion would be lost if someone went behind the curtain and saw all the debris stored away out of public sight: cleaning fluid; a spare cross with a mosaic Jesus on it; some wilting plastic flowers and a convector radiator, on the last viewing.

When it's not a client getting in touch with strange requests, the rest of my calls tend to be arrangers from one of the local funeral directors that use me regularly. Social calls these days are few and far between: people have given up trying to arrange things, as the irregular patterns of work have made me unreliable.

It's almost impossible to plan ahead. A new booking coming in can throw the week's diary in an instant and the last-minute nature of the requests, delivered in pleading tones from the arrangers, usually see to that.

"Please can you see this lovely family urgently. They all live in different parts of the country and are only together for a couple of days. Go on pleeeeeeeease," one of them begged. "Give them a call now and see if you can pop over."

And so I did. We all do, it's just part of the job.

This has seen me, amongst other things cancelling nights out and dates; even delaying my holiday departure; arriving in picturesque Wales in the dead of night, when I should have been on the beach, sunning my freckles at midday.

But the client will never know the personal investment we make, because it's our choice to do this work, and it's not for us to burden them with any of it.

Sometimes however, the phone rings and it's totally different news. Not a request, and not a booking; like the time Sarah from one of the local Co-Op funeral branches called.

"Sorry Ruth," she said. "Just a quick one to say the family didn't like you. They want a male celebrant now instead."

And there it was; un-sugar-coated; un-adulterated rejection; just two hours after meeting them all. Exactly what I didn't need on top of blocked drains and a 5lb weight gain.

Sarah petered out, not really knowing what to say, so it was me that ended up waffling: "Okay! An unbooking it is. Ha, ha! Never mind, these things happen. Good job I've got a thick skin!" I was aware of sounding slightly manic; no wonder she couldn't get off the phone quick enough.

Afterwards, I reflected on how that would have made me feel in the early days of my career. It wasn't pleasant eight years down the line, but in the first year or so, that would have been enough to knock my confidence almost completely.

I found out much later that call was also on the back of a bad morning for poor Sarah. She'd had issues with a family claiming the ashes in the urn she'd given them weren't their dad. Apparently he'd been a big man and they were convinced it should have weighed more!

She'd also had a very angry Father McMahon on the phone ranting about his overdue payment. Hell certainly hath no fury like a priest unpaid!

But back to my unceremonious dismissal.

I had slightly suspected things weren't going well at the meet with the four siblings (three women and one man).

The youngest sister had been so grief-stricken she couldn't speak. The two older sisters sat in a huddle, *literally* pointing at me like children, whispering behind their hands to each other as if I wasn't there.

This left the poor brother to do all the talking, whilst being contradicted by all three of them. They couldn't even seem to agree on where they'd lived as children.

The only thing they did settle upon was the music:

'Wind Beneath My Wings' by Bette Midler to come in to; 'Time To Say Goodbye' by Sarah Brightman for reflection; and for the exit, that evergreen classic 'Unforgettable' by Nat King Kong.

I tried really hard, but I think I may have snorted at that.

"Do you mean Nat King Cole?"

All four of them had turned to glare at that point. The atmosphere became tangibly frosty, so I guess that's where I'd lost them totally.

Mulling it over later, I did feel a bit miffed. I'd taken copious notes in a very uncomfortable atmosphere, and behaved totally professionally, apart from the snort.

I'd used my previous experience in journalism to really dig underneath the shallowest of details they'd provided in order to get some proper information on their dad. The service would have been all the fuller and more rounded had I been able to use it, but it wasn't to be. As Sarah said, they didn't like me, and that was that.

This was one of the things we covered whilst learning how to become a celebrant; the potential for difficult meetings or even hostility on a family visit.

Our trainer put it another way asking, 'What's in the family's bucket?' Grief? Anger? Hopelessness? Despair? Indifference? Hostility? And what is in ours when we go? Professionalism; empathy; kindness;

people skills; time-management; patience; writing skills; a genuine curiosity and liking for people and a desire to do your very best to give someone a personal and sincere goodbye in order to allow those left behind to heal.

That's the intent anyway, and the vast majority of the time it goes more than well. Occasionally, as in the afore-mentioned example, it can get a bit sticky for some unknown reason.

The other danger area is when a family is divided, and one of them assumes 'client' status, leaving the un-favoured family members out of the picture. This is not an uncommon occurrence, but it puts us celebrants in a hugely difficult situation.

To explain, the hierarchy is thus: we are freelance self-employed contractors, and get our bookings directly from the funeral arrangers in most cases.

We then contact the client (known as the 'chief mourner') and make arrangements to visit the family. The client is the person we take instructions from, as they're the ones contracted with the FD and the people who will be paying the final bill.

At the family visit, the aim is to pull together the order of service (OOS), what it will contain, and also to gather up all the details of the deceased in order to write a sparkling, meaningful and reflective eulogy.

This is great if a family gets on; if the conversation flows and there's plenty to write about. Not so great if one family member has pulled rank over the others and not even told them about the meeting with me!

This happened in autumn 2022 when I went to meet Sally to talk about her dad. She gave me a fair amount of information about his unremarkable life; so even as she spoke I was mentally reaching for my 'Not Done A Lot But Was Reasonably Liked' folder; shaping up the service in my head as she chatted away.

It would be a fairly standard start probably. Something like:

'It's safe to say that Bruce lived an ordinary life, but not all of us are born to lead nations and change the world. The most important thing is that he did things his way, choosing his own path and that he harmed nobody in the process. Bruce never had a bad word to say about anyone. Wouldn't it be wonderful if we could all say the same for ourselves?'

And from there I'd talk about the family, his legacy of kindness, put it all into perspective and job done! So I asked about the family of course, and was told by Sally that she had 'some' brothers, but as they hadn't bothered with dad for years they didn't need a mention and they wouldn't be there.

I probed a little: was she absolutely sure they wouldn't be? Did I need to contact them for their perspective at least?

No, she assured me – they were a fractured family; absolutely impossible to pin down so it was all best left in her capable hands.

I left the meeting with a feeling of foreboding, which proved timely. After writing the service and getting it approved by Sally I got an email from one of the brothers.

'Hello," it said. "My name is Eddie Barker, son of Bruce for who you is (sic) doing a service. Me and my brothers are not happy that my sister has taken over. She showed us your words and what you have written is not his proper life story. Please contact me urgently to put this straight.'

It was just two days before the funeral. My heart wanted to call Eddie and get his side of the story, but my head implored me not to. Based on a previous experience when I tried to appease two sides of a warring family (which ended up in a formal complaint; a threat by the family to 'expose' me as a fraud to the local papers, and being blacklisted by that particular FD), I just couldn't get involved.

I ignored the email but called Sally immediately. "Your brother has been in touch. He's unhappy with the eulogy; says it's not reflective of your dad's life."

She swore, following it up with "Leave it with me. I'll text you later with some amends."

The text came in at 10.30 pm. I was to add in all the grandchildren's names (not just her daughter; he actually had twelve grandchildren!), and I was also to erase dad's move to the seaside; fifteen years of his life just wiped way.

At the time I thought that strange. Why erase such a huge portion of time? I later found out it was during this period he'd been suspected of indecent exposure to a child, so no wonder they wanted that bit of his history gone! The final amendment was to add in some more family memories from the brothers.

All this was duly done first thing in the morning, the day before the funeral. It was signed off once more by Sally and I breathed a sigh of relief. I could get on with my other family meetings and writing knowing this one was in the bag at last.

Wrong!

I got a further email from Eddie that night whilst I was out having a meal. He felt the need to tell me I'd been an unhelpful cow. Didn't I know he was grieving too and I'd made it all the worse by ignoring his email and not letting him see the final draft of the service?

Ignoring the insult I toyed again with writing to Eddie, explaining the dilemma and saying as a human being yes, I totally understood his frustration. He'd lost his dad and needed that goodbye to be 'right' for him too. But did *he* understand what huge trouble I'd be in if his sister (the all-powerful 'client') decided to make a formal complaint should I dare to circumnavigate her instructions, and deal directly with him?

No, he probably wouldn't have understood. And as a grieving son he probably wouldn't have cared. Therefore, although it's dreadfully unpleasant, I always remind myself that misplaced fury is a hazard of the job, and it's more than balanced out by the majority of families who are delightful, decent people just grateful to have someone there to assist them; even if every request, like the puppet, can't always be accommodated.

CHAPTER 3: THE HARDEST GOODBYE

I found my mother weeping on her bed one day when I was twenty-three. When I asked her why, she simply replied, "Today would have been Alison's birthday."

That was the first mention I'd ever heard of this piece of news. Who on earth was Alison? And more importantly, why did my mum have such an attachment to her?

The story tumbled out. Of how she'd carried the child before me with such excitement. She remembered writing a letter to a friend just a week before the due date, saying how in a week's time, she'd have a baby in her arms.

Just twenty four hours, the day before delivery, her baby stopped moving. She'd been strangled by the cord. And so my mum delivered her dead child, which was taken away in a metal bucket; un-held, un-named and never spoken of again. She never even got to see her face.

Had I been born today, I'd have been called a rainbow baby; the name coined for a healthy arrival after a previous child is lost to miscarriage, stillbirth, or neonatal death.

Sadly, back in 1962, the profession had no time for such nonsense, for the softening of bad news. Birth was dealt with practically, with no partners in attendance. And as for a baby's loss? Well, that was swept under the carpet with an 'Oh well, you can always try again,' kind of attitude.

I've thought of that moment often; wondered frequently if Alison had made it, would mother have had a happier life? Would I have? She was pregnant with me just six weeks after the loss: barely any time to recover. I was made in a womb full of grief.

Rainbow baby or not, I didn't bring colour or happiness to her life. Her heart was calcified; her breasts remained empty and I guess it was just all too soon. Sadly, the bond never went on to form.

Enough years have passed for all of this to be put into perspective, but what does remain is the memory of her sadness, still so intense after twenty three years. And that is one of the reasons I say 'yes' when I get an enquiry to take a baby funeral service. I've seen first-hand the effects of loss when it's badly-handled; and I want to do better for people.

Another reason is the fact celebrants are not clergy, bound by dogma, tradition or expectations of religious context. We're free to produce a totally unique service in a way that can, if it's managed with sensitivity and kindness, truly affect a family's recovery and their potential for future happiness.

Having said that, from the moment I take the booking, through to the initial tortuous phone call to mum and dad, and on to the funeral day, it's a massive burden. Feeling the parents' grief, combined with the responsibility of getting everything 'just so' is enormous and yes, of course it takes its toll.

As a very small gesture, the officiant will generally waive their fees for anybody under sixteen years of age; it's the least we can do. It just wouldn't seem right asking for money in such utterly tragic circumstances. All thoughts of earning a living go out of the window, in favour of making things a little more bearable for the families in such trauma.

It's only in recent years that funerals for the loss of a child have extended to include babies 'born sleeping'; and even babies classed as a non-viable foetus. The funeral industry is all the better for this. Alongside the actual death, it also acknowledges the loss of hope, of futures that will never unfold. And by allowing parents a 'proper' funeral, regardless of the circumstances, it gives them a platform upon which they can build and start over.

The army of others involved in changing the landscape keep on working too. Like the amazing people at one particular funeral parlour where they have a dedicated 'Lullaby Room' for parents to spend their time with the baby before the final goodbye.

This room contains a discreetly refrigerated Cuddle-Cot, beautifully dressed just like the real thing. As one of the directors said to me, "It's just so important that they can create these memories to cling to."

For evidence, should I have needed it, he then went on to tell me about the family who camped out there for three days.

"It's no exaggeration," he continued, "to say they were on the doorstep at 9am. They couldn't wait to get in.

"We gave them breakfast and lunch. We kept them watered all day. But most importantly, we kept them together."

My colleague Sharon is another major cog in this process around the Birmingham and West-Midlands area of the UK too. This amazing lady recognised the importance of babies, no matter what their size, having something decent to wear for their send off.

She's right too. We think nothing of taking a final outfit to the funeral directors for an adult to wear do we? Knowing our loved one is dressed properly is one of the boxes we tick when preparations are being made. We can say, 'Ah yes, he looked lovely in his wedding suit/favourite football top/most comfy dressing gown, and that's how we will remember him.'

But for babies, that's generally not so. Too often parents have seen their little one in a scrap of hospital fabric; and that's been their parting and lasting memory.

This has partly been down to the archaic attitudes mentioned previously, and also the fact it would have been impossible to dress a baby under twenty weeks, as they're not developed enough. But now, thanks to Sharon, parents get a chance to see their child looking beautiful; and the importance of this cannot be under-estimated.

The process begins at Sharon's house, as she collects and launders unwanted wedding dresses. It's not unusual to visit and find two or three of them drying on the line, whilst inside the kitchen there are boxes and boxes containing pink and blue fasteners and metres and metres of ribbon and edging. Rolls of elastic sit side by side with teddy bear fur, tiny little heart buttons and imitation pearls.

These are then dispatched to an army of volunteer seamstresses who transform the wedding dresses into doll-sized outfits, which ultimately make their way back to Sharon.

Sharon then personally distributes these beautiful sets of clothing, sized accordingly, to the funeral directors who currently hold the 'baby contracts' for the council. And so the little trousers and caps; T-shirts and dresses, ceremonial gowns, bracelets and tiny teddies find their owners, and together they make their way to their final resting place.

All this is done at Sharon's own expense and in her own time, so it's no surprise she's won several national celebrancy awards for her work along the way.

Sadly, the last baby service I conducted was for a little girl who was more than able to wear her own clothing as she was two years old.

I met her parents at home; a lovely young couple in their thirties, it was one of the most difficult meetings ever; but we got there in the end.

They cried a lot and supported each other when they needed it. We watched videos of their baby learning to toddle, and riding her trike, shrieking with delight as she rolled down the garden path. And again as she attempted to sit on the long-suffering dog's back.

They showed me her playroom, everything neatly stacked away. Her father stood in the doorway with me and just shook his head. All he could manage at that point was, "It's such a shame."

I wanted to sob. To really cling to the door frame and just howl. For these poor people and their pain and struggle. For my mother's twenty-three year silence. For all the people who never got a decent goodbye.

Sometimes it just builds up, we're only human. But then I have to remember the promise we made to ourselves when training. To not get involved. That this is not our grief and if we make it ours, not only are we robbing the family of their moment, but we're not doing our job. Getting too involved means we aren't being effective.

And so I pulled myself together and got planning. And although it was utterly heart-breaking, the service was beautiful.

On the day, the chapel was decked out with balloons and streamers but even with such efforts I could hardly bear to watch daddy stagger in, bowed under the emotional weight of the tiny white teddy-bear coffin.

I spoke a few words and recounted the little girl's story to date. And then, in accordance with mum's wishes that we put her child to bed rather than send-her off, I read her a goodnight story.

I said to the family that I'd leave them alone in the chapel for a while at that point. They were listening to the lullaby 'Hushabye Mountain' from the film Chitty Chitty Bang Bang, and I wanted them to have their final moments together without me.

I did cry outside as I was waiting, but fortunately managed to pull myself together when the family came out. But honestly? There were no more words. We just smiled wanly and went our separate ways.

CHAPTER 4: THE PAST AND THE PRESENT

Dealing with the work is a challenge, of course it is. There's definitely emotional fallout and it tends to build up year on year. Thank goodness there's a private online forum that many of us share.

Always a constant source of inspiration, knowledge and humour we use it to decompress; empathise and sympathise, but no matter how supportive the forum, a virtual hug can never replace the real thing.

That physical touch and support has definitely been missing for the majority of my career. The pain of the funerals weighs heavy without someone to listen; and the happiness of others' weddings has always been slightly diluted by the spotlight shining on the lack of love in my own life. It's no exaggeration to say that sometimes I've literally ached for a loyal pair of arms to slough the weight of it all away. Sadly though, love and I have never been a great match.

Growing up in what would best be described as a neglectful environment, I didn't get the dose of self-esteem that kids need to become fully-rounded adults, able amongst other things, to choose a future partner wisely.

I can't describe the humiliation of a teacher contacting my mother to tell her she needed to buy me a bra (I was size 34C when I got my first one). And it's impossible to convey how being put down on a daily basis can send one's internal compass so askew.

Her final, cruel blow was to call me to her bedside to hear her dying words. Thinking there'd be some sort of reconciliation, I practically flew there. But again, I was disappointed.

"Don't get married and don't have children, it's not worth it," was not what I needed to hear.

It wouldn't take Sherlock Holmes to deduce that such bad treatment wasn't great for my mental health; and it did send me off at a tangent for many years, seeking approval and love in the wrong places. Happily though, it's something I've at last been able to forgive myself for.

Notable mistakes have included a French man called Eric who used to write me adoring letters on notepaper with an embossed picture of a stallion rearing up on it. The kind of paper a thirteen year old girl would have doodled dreamily on in the 1970s.

In his immature scrawl Eric would gush out his feelings, saying things like 'I love beautiful girl with blue eye.' Letters were often signed off with the perplexing declaration, 'I hamp you very strang.'

Eric was a manifestation of my low self-esteem: a kind of 'he'll do because nobody else is interested', choice. But the worst was probably Vinnie. A man of mixed temperament, he came from a once-thriving coal mining town in the West Midlands where, for hundreds of years, sons had followed fathers into the pits.

That's all gone now, and like many other areas, it's turned into an aimless infrastructure of supermarkets, closed down shops and affordable new-build housing estates that curiously, nobody seems very keen to ever leave.

Vinnie was no different. He wasn't bright, educated, worldly or in the least bit curious to step over the town's borders. Any attempt to strike up conversation about current affairs or the arts was met with the standard response; 'You know your trouble? You think too much.'

I should have expected nothing more from a man whose favourite saying was, 'Cannock born, Cannock bred; thick in arm and thick in head,' but in my usual shallow way I'd been drawn in by those dashing blue eyes and long dark hair.

To me Vinnie looked like a pop star from the eighties. My friend said he displayed more feral cunning than a weasel, but either way, if I'm honest, I probably saw him more as an exciting challenge. As someone to be reformed through exploring the big wide world together.

Vinnie was another classic low self-esteem choice. I saw it as my mission to save him (even though he seemed quite happy with who he was), but I figured if I could show him new things and seem interesting, then perhaps he'd need me more.

Vinnie had other ideas. The suggestion of a trip to London one weekend brought the response: "London. Fecking London? What are you talking about? My brother's pub's on the doorstep; work's three minutes away and the garage across the road does kebabs. It's all 'ere!"

I should have ended it then. I knew in my heart it wasn't right. The man lived in a leaking caravan almost on top of a traffic roundabout for God's sake. What had he really got to offer? But no, I stuck it out. There were still more delights to come.

Like the time he took me out for a meal to a Toby Carvery (a kind of meat and two-veg buffet) where you're served by a sweating man in a chef's hat behind the counter.

We made small talk and chased peas around our plate. At the end of the meal I remarked that Vinnie had a spot of gravy on his chin.

"Thanks for telling me," he said, then leaned over to seamlessly wipe his face *on the restaurant curtains!!* This was topped only by him picking his teeth with a £10 note, before using it to pay the bill.

Frozen with horror I toyed with just leaving, there and then. Instead, three weeks later, I agreed to get engaged. I was almost forty and never wed. Time was running out.

Too embarrassed to tell anybody, I crept with him into Birmingham's Jewellery Quarter one Boxing Day, him figuring there would be a bargain to be had in the post-Christmas sales.

Surprisingly there was just one shop open, so naturally we went in to make our selection. I wanted something simple and non-expensive. Maybe just a platinum ring with a small solitaire diamond.

When we walked through the door, the man behind the counter looked startled. He was tidying away the shelves looking very distracted.

There was barely any stock on show and at a quick glance it was all just trays of gold rings.

Placing my hand expectantly on the counter I said: "We've just got engaged."

The man ignored us and carried on packing away.

I continued: "So I'd like something simple please. Not the gold things that are out. Maybe something just platinum, with a small diamond?"

He shot me the briefest of glances.

"We've got nothing for those ugly hands," was the instant reply.

The moment froze in time whilst Vinnie and I processed it. Then Vinnie leapt into action. "You what? You fecking what?"

"I told you," said the jeweller. "We've nothing for those hands."

It's no exaggeration to say I had to drag Vinnie from the shop, spitting and clawing at the air, muttering all kinds of threats. In the end, the only thing that distracted him from his fury was a Greggs steak bake pasty.

I remember standing a distance away, watching Vinnie snapping at the pastry aggressively, muttering to himself as he chewed. The picture of him sat open-legged and open-mouthed on a bench, crumbs falling all around as the pigeons gathered at his feet will stay with me forever.

As will the memory of my escalating regret at tying myself to such an idiot. But it already felt too late to change my mind.

We returned to the Jewellery Quarter the next day to complete the mission and ended up in a shop almost opposite the one we'd visited the previous day.

I chatted to the assistant as we chose my bargain ball and chain. "Oh," I told her, "We tried to get a ring from that place yesterday. But the man wasn't very helpful."

She looked at me aghast for a moment then burst out laughing. "I'm not surprised," she said, "the shop was burgled yesterday! Do you think you may have interrupted it?"

It didn't bode well, that we'd attempted to get engaged during a robbery. And so it proved to be. Vinnie wasn't for reforming or educating. I wasn't up for a life in a leaking mobile home eating garage kebabs, being told my trouble was that I thought too much.

Looking back, I gleaned a lot from that relationship, the most important thing being that it's most certainly better to be single than to compromise to such an extent. Unsurprisingly, it was with much relief that we eventually went our separate ways.

And so it remained for several years. I ploughed my solitary furrow, enjoyed my friends and my lovely gruff little terrier Gloria, and just got on with it. Going it alone wasn't so bad; I was honestly in the zone where I was prepared to continue that way for the rest of my life. But then some friends mooted that I may like to meet a friend of theirs called Russ who'd been widowed six months previously?

Ironically, although I didn't know it, they'd originally suggested to Russ that I conducted his wife's funeral. In hindsight, it's probably a good thing that never happened, as dating someone from those circumstances would have been sheer awkward. (Then again, I do know one couple who literally met over a dead body in a mortuary, and they've been married sixteen years!)

But there he was; this kind, quietly humorous, considerate and yes handsome man, who'd found himself single through no fault of his own.

I told him on our first date that I thought he was incredibly brave. I also needed to check that he was ready to see somebody again, with things being so soon. His response moved me deeply.

"Look Ruth," he said sadly, "I could wear black and mourn for a year or two, just to satisfy everyone that I was truly depressed and down.

"But after the service you know what? Everyone went back to their normal lives and it was just me and the boys. Mum shared some easy family recipes to help me cope with the cooking; the neighbours popped round with some cake once or twice, and that was it.

"And then," he continued, "I had to make a choice. Did I want this gaping emptiness for the rest of my life? Absolutely not! So having made that decision, I wasn't going to hang around for the sake of somebody else's perception of 'decency'. I just thought I needed to get on with it while I was still relatively young. It's not easy to meet someone else. I'd anticipated it may take a good while so I took a deep breath, and here we are."

I know from experience, catching up with the odd ex-client occasionally that men do tend to move on faster than women. I don't think they are as independent as we are, and need the company more, so Russ's words didn't surprise me.

What did surprise me over the next few subsequent meetings though, was how easy it all was. How the conversation just flowed, and with so much laughter.

This ease wouldn't have suited me thirty or even twenty years ago. Back then I thought love had to hurt. That it had to be fought for or surrounded by drama, passion or crisis. That I had to try really hard to be entertaining, useful, sexy or mysterious.

All of that thankfully changed on meeting Russ. As things slowly moved forwards I realised I was finally ready for respect and kindness; a soft place to land.

Another bonus was the fact he was local. Near enough to just pop in and see when I was passing on my rounds. It was on one of those visits that I produced a copy of my first book for him to read.

I thought it was pretty ballsy of me at such an early stage, as it's a warts and all memoir. He'd know about all my previous jobs; my awful family life with mum and dad; the disastrous relationships and, equally importantly, how much of a toll the work takes on me. But I figured it was better to get things out of the way sooner rather than later: he needed to know who I was and see the imperfections. If he was going to bail, I wanted it to be before anyone got deeply hurt.

I got a text the next day. It simply said "I'm so proud of you."

I may have burst into tears. Gloria sat there obligingly, letting me cry into her fur as I stroked her, mumbling something like 'I think it's going to be okay Glo. I don't think we're on our own any more.'

Months down the line Russ recalled how he'd felt reading the book and getting to know me further. Again, he said something beautiful.

"When I met you Ruth and heard all your sad stories, I could see how much all that struggle had affected you. My first instinct was to fix you.

"But as things progressed I came to realise you're the most capable person I've ever met. You don't need fixing. You're wild and bohemian and creative and inspiring. I think maybe all you need is some love; from someone who is going to stick around. And if you'll let me do that, when you're ready, I'll be there."

That's what I alluded to at the end of the first book. That someone had stepped into my life and it was looking hopeful. It still is. He's constantly there, loving me through weight loss and gain; different hairstyles and colours. He's there, taking the wine glass out of my hand when I've gone a bit daft and lost sight of the fact that extra measure will give me a headache in the morning.

He's there to put another log on the fire when I'm cold (in fact he'll go outside to get the logs) and he's my permanent cheerleader through the ups and downs.

Although we don't live together, for my part I try my hardest to support him too, particularly when it comes to his twin boys who were just fourteen years old when we met.

Not at all alike, Kyle and Aaron also have very different personalities. Kyle is super-bright, self-regulating, studious and very close to his dad. Aaron is much more independent, harder to motivate and less willing to help out, but he's quick witted and can get by on his charm (when he wants to pull it out of the bag).

They most definitely don't come as a matching pair, but the one thing they both shared (although it hadn't been acknowledged at the time), was a need to start doing more for themselves; to be less dependent on dad for absolutely everything. In brief, they needed to grow up.

It was plain Russ and his wife had doted on their boys, but as a result they didn't know how to boil an egg; change a bed; go into a shop and order a coffee or even go to the hairdresser's on their own. They didn't even think for themselves – every single little thing had been facilitated, organised and provided.

To someone who has had a job and been almost self-sufficient since the age of twelve, that came as a real shock. Consequently Russ and I had many conversations (heated and otherwise) over the next year, during which I tried to encourage him to let go a little. To let them do things for themselves and make a few mistakes, knowing dad would always be there to support them regardless.

A timetable got drawn up for chores, and then forgotten about, with Russ sighing and saying it was easier to get on with things himself as he knew they'd be done properly. I pinned it back on the wall and reminded Aaron it was his turn to load the dishwasher that week.

I'd stepped into this co-dependant threesome and it wasn't always welcome, but I became an expert at ignoring the clipped responses and occasional but deliberate silences from the boys. I also kept reminding Russ how vital it was for them to be learning new skills and taking responsibilities, and that it would, it really would, pay off in the end.

At this stage I'm sure you may be thinking 'Well what does a childless woman in her fifties know about parenting? Not much as it happens, but I do have a lot of common sense. And I have a background where rules and boundaries changed weekly. I know how it feels to be insecure because the right framework isn't in place.

Some days I was in favour, other times I'd be ignored for a week. Sometimes I could go out with my friends, and others mum would tell them I was already out, or just busy (usually doing piles of the family's ironing, in truth.)

This see-saw existence did nothing but ensure I never knew where I stood. It also made me realise in adulthood that kids *do* need to be doing things for themselves within a structure of guidance and boundaries. But it needs to be consistent. They have to understand that no means no. And they need rewards when things are being done well.

If you're still not convinced as to my credentials, then I could pull out of the bag the story of the time I worked at a holiday park for an entire season where (quite inexplicably), I found myself in charge of a hundred or more kids every single week!

From kids' club on a Saturday (when the entire mob would pour though the door as one, screaming for their club magazine, their free T-shirts and the candies); right through to running the entertainments and discos, I look back on that experience as formative, exhausting and very useful. Additionally it sealed the decision never to have any monsters of my own!

I also realised that kids of eight to twelve are no different from those of sixteen. They all push boundaries and test the water. They all need time, attention and love. And they all need to feel secure. For Russ's boys, losing their mother so early in their lives can't fail to have undone that feeling.

It's a work in progress, and will continue to be for a while, but we're getting there. Kyle is learning to cook. The chore chart remains on the wall. We've stayed the odd night away from home and left the boys to it: the house wasn't burnt down and there were no wild parties. We're all learning as we go along, but things are moving in the right direction.

Perhaps though it's me who's learnt the biggest lesson of all so far. The lesson of how incredible it is that one can wither so thoroughly under the shadow of distain, but blossom so beautifully, through being valued and loved.

CHAPTER 5: WITH THIS CELEBRANT I THEE WED

On the subject of love, that brings me to the happier side of a celebrant's work where we get the joy and privilege of helping couples enjoy the best days of their lives; the weddings.

In Australia a celebrant can marry a couple legally. In the UK it's more of a symbolic ceremony, but if a couple can separate out their thinking and understand that the ceremony (anything from the love letters; vows; rings; candle lighting; family participation and more) is the actual wedding – then we're on! The signing is purely admin day, and that can be done separately from the actual occasion.

Another way of explaining it is like this: all of our big events in life (births, deaths and marriages) have the happening and then the registration. A baby is born (the event), it's recorded. Someone dies (the event), it's recorded. And the same for a marriage. The couple make their vows and do whatever else they want to do in front of witnesses; and then it's registered later to legalise the ceremony. When put like this, most couples then totally get the value of having a celebrant, as it offers so much scope to do things personally.

Before we came along, the only options were to have a fully-religious service in a church (or similar) or to get married in a Register Office, which is a little less formal but still very restrictive as to what is allowed. And how dull is that? Particularly when you consider that the ceremony is generally conducted with the couple's backs to the congregation!

All of that changes when a celebrant comes in, ready to create something meaningful, personal and unique for every couple.

I tend to attract quirky, fun people who don't take life too seriously. Whilst there's always a central more serious part to the service around the vows and rings, (it does have to have some gravitas to make it meaningful); the rest of the service can be as fun and light-hearted as required. Then, if they haven't done it beforehand, the couple slip off a day or so later to get on with admin day; a basic service at the registry office which should cost around £50.

Interestingly enough, this is exactly how an Islamic marriage works in the UK. Their service, the one upon which the entire marriage is based, is called the Nikah. In the eyes of Islam, it's a 'real' marriage, but as it's not recognised in UK law, they still have to legalise it at the Register Office.

The Register Office basic service that I suggest to my couples isn't advertised widely because it's not their most profitable offering, but it's there if you know what to ask for.

Sometimes it's packaged as a basic service; other times it's sold under the banner of a bronze package, but either way it literally takes just a few minutes. And that's because the only part that makes the whole thing legal, is what's called the 'Declaratory and Contracting Statements'.

That's the bits where each partner declares they're free to marry: (I x solemnly declare I know not of any lawful impediment why I should not be joined in matrimony to y).

And then the contracting words: (I call upon these persons present to witness that I x take you y to be my lawful wedded husband/wife). The only other requirement is that two witnesses are present; and that's about it. No need to pay for a big room, flowers or a beautiful view, and that's why I advise everyone to save all the 'good stuff' for the ceremony with me, where it really matters.

So if you want to get married with a celebrant in a woodland, then that's entirely possible. Or at home in the garden; in a friend's field, or at the restaurant where you had your first date – that's fine. You want religion, or no religion – that's also fine. You want your family to get up and sing; or an ancient hand-fasting ceremony, or a symbolic ceremony like a tree planting? Yes – that's all good too. The important thing is planning, a solid script and a sense of fun.

All of these came to the fore in the wedding for Susan and Jack, who also wanted to combine a 'family blending' ceremony. Jack had taken on Susan's two daughters when they met, and he wanted to publicly acknowledge his commitment to all of them as individuals, and the new family unit being created.

Despite Susan's dress being so wide that I had to stand some way apart from them; and the sun shining in my eyes so I could hardly read the script, everything went superbly, with the added bonus of lots of impromptu laughter at the couple's story as I told it.

We were striking all the right chords and it was going beautifully and then it came to symbolic part of the service where everyone involved took up a personalised vial of coloured sand to pour into a bigger vase, with the family name and wedding date engraved upon it.

I'll share this part of the script if I may:

"Now this lovely couple have been joined in matrimony, it's time to complete the family circle and involve the children Stacey and Louise in the final ceremony.

"Jack has loved and cherished the girls as his own since coming into their lives. And in turn, they have come to adore him too.

"As part of each other's lives, the girls will in effect be part of this marriage. The solidifying of this new family will have a deep influence upon them.

"Everyone wanted to reflect this through the symbolism of a sand ceremony, where the pouring of these individual containers of sand into one, signifies the change of status: from separate individuals to one bonded family.

"So I'm going to call up Stacey to pour her sand in first. The red represents the passion for family and the energy within these four relationships.

"And now Louise: she has the green sand to represent fresh elements and a curiosity to try new things. We see green in nature every spring as things renew.

"For Susan, she's chosen the champagne colour: not her words, but I reckon it's perfect for such a bubbly person.

"And finally Jack, who has chosen blue for honesty, loyalty and strength within the relationship.

"As you combine your sand together, your lives also join together as one family. Just as these grains of sand can never be separated and poured again into the individual containers, so will your marriage and your family be.

"And there we have this beautiful reminder of this special day and how everyone is inter-connected and part of the bigger picture. May your lives together be blessed and may you be always surrounded with the sense of love and belonging that is in the room today."

At that, several women burst into tears and a spontaneous round of applause erupted. You don't get that with a council registry office wedding, and *that's* why people choose a celebrant.

Another couple that stood out for different reasons were Gemma and Murray. They lived in New Zealand but were returning to the UK to be married in her family woodland.

Over the months we chatted, first by phone then online, I got the measure of them as a couple and as individuals. Both world travellers concerned with saving the planet, they wanted to re-connect with their friends and family, and for this reason it was important to involve everyone as much as possible in the service.

They were great fun too: they wanted to strike the balance between sincerity, commitment and warm laughter, and they also wanted to include an element of surprise. This was answered firstly by factoring the dog Hendrix into the service as the 'ring bearer', and secondly by writing secret love letters for each other, to be read out before the vows and exchange of rings.

It was all sounding fantastic, even before the addition of a gospel choir, and a Pied Piper to lead everyone through the woodland up to the service!

I was just taking it all in, when Gemma said, "You're a musician Ruth. Do you know anyone who could play the role? We see the piper with a flute, in character. A cheerful, cheeky kind of chap. Is this a tall order do you think?"

As it happened, on that particular day, it wasn't. My friend Jobe sprung immediately to mind. He's only 23, but he plays eight instruments and is possibly the most connected musician I've ever known. And the most random; the job was made for him.

And that's how we both found ourselves in a set of portaloos in the Worcestershire countryside, sweltering in the August heat as we changed into our respective outfits.

For me it was a floaty, hippie-type dress and sandals. And for red-head Jobe it was red, green and yellow felt trousers; a matching tunic; a ruff around his neck; a green beret; flowing lace cuffs (think 'Meatloaf'), and a fetching little green drawstring bag.

We wrestled with the hook and eye attachment to the ruff for a good while, but then it dawned on me that he probably couldn't have looked any more ridiculous if he'd tried; the effect was already complete. So, we ditched the unwanted bit of rogue lace and got ourselves outside to start taking photos with which to amuse ourselves later.

Pictures duly taken, we then strolled around the field, taking in the scenery. Aside from the portaloos, there was an area for outdoor games (obviously entertainment for later), and a huge tipi, beautifully laid out for dinner with crystal glasses, china plates and exquisite floral arrangements. There was also a large bar, a dance floor, and a small stage, where the gospel choir was rehearsing.

We milled around a little, me bathed in a fine sheen of menopausal sweat, and Jobe melting in sympathy with me from inside his felt tunic. Then, it was time to peel off and begin the proceedings.

Jobe's mission was to round up the guests, and 'pipe' his way to the ceremony. The plan was that by the time he'd got everyone together, I'd be in position, along with the choir to start it all.

Like I say, that was the plan. But first of all, I had to get myself there. My sense of direction isn't great at the best of times (I once lost my bearings in a friend's hallway. She only has five rooms, and I couldn't find the front door). So yes, there was me in the woodland, unable to find the site for the service.

In my defence, I'd envisaged something like an orchard, not the 250 acres of dense trees, brambles and ferns that I found myself wandering through. I tried several of the distinct pathways, wide enough to drive a four by four through, but I couldn't seem to find the right one.

Every time I thought I was going somewhere, it led to the logging yard, or the curious little 'gingerbread house' in the clearing. After multiple attempts to find the wedding site, my dress was trailing on the brambles, my legs were getting scratched and my flip flop-style shoes weren't staying on. And I was dying for a pee again.

Things always feel easier without being hampered by a full bladder, so I decided to take advantage of the solitude and squat down in the ferns for a moment.

All was going well until I was startled by a baby fallow deer, which caused me to jerk upwards, mid-stream, soaking the hem of my dress. Honestly, I could have wept. It was feeling less and less like the magical day I'd hoped, and more like 'I'm A Celebrant Get Me Out Of Here'.

Fortunately, I then heard Jobe's piping drifting through the woods. Very faint, but it was there; I'd have to follow him instead. Fifteen minutes later, he appeared, ashen faced and sweating. 'Annie's song' (no doubt chosen for the words, 'you fill up my senses, like a night in the forest'), was sounding more like a staccato Irish jig, as Jobe alternately played and gasped for breath.

Next time you see an orchestra play, contrast the comfort of the flautist playing from a seat, with poor Jobe, who had just walked for twenty minutes up steep inclines and down slopes, all whilst expelling air into his flute. No surprise then, when we finally got to the allotted site, he flung himself down on a log, panting like a stunned mullet, just as the gospel choir burst into song.

What a welcome! We'd made it! A year in the planning, and here we were, standing in the specially-prepared clearing on the viewing platform, with a backdrop of country views stretching over to Worcestershire's Malvern Hills. I swear, despite the searing heat, goose bumps of pleasure popped up all over my arms.

When everyone had settled on their felled tree trunks (with cushions on top for comfort), there was another song, which everyone was encouraged to join in, and then some banter between the audience and the bridegroom Murray.

Just as that was coming to an end, we heard the roar of engines, and the hooting of horns as the bride arrived in her own safari jeep, along with the wedding party. And so, to applause and cheers, the best day of their lives began.

When it came to the love letters before the vows and rings, (the ones they'd prepared in secret), there wasn't a dry eye in the house, especially at Gemma's wonderful line to Murray.

Speaking of their adventures and travels together, she said, "I've seen the best of you, and the worst of you; and I choose both."

What a fantastically honest and realistic approach to a marriage. That line stayed with me for weeks afterward: I choose both. It echoed of maturity and honesty, and it got me thinking about the nature of marriage and relationships in general.

I may be comfortable around marriage in terms of working with couples to create a great service; but I'd never considered it seriously for myself. Every time I even began to wonder if I ever would, old fears and well-worn excuses leapt to the fore. Things like, 'I'm used to my own space'; 'I like doing things my way'; 'I need my sleep' …

I remember e-mailing a similarly love-jaded friend to ask some advice many years back. My then partner was kind and considerate, but we had nothing in common. I told her I couldn't envisage future years sipping wine as we watched the sunset, him talking about football until my eyes glazed over with boredom. But with my chances dwindling year on year, I asked her if I should take what was currently on offer? A kind but imperfect man who was deadly serious and with whom I never laughed?

Here's what she replied:

"Oh! You're thinking of marriage? Well, that's a surprise. Sounds to me like you're not convinced it's right for you. If you went ahead I'd be pleased of course, but just make sure, because getting out of it is an awful faff ..."

That made me laugh. Twenty years ago, she'd have been all bells, whistles, streamers and congratulations. Two husbands, two kids and several rescue greyhounds later, she's had a dose of reality.

But at least she's been able to make that judgement from the perspective of a normal life in a normal setting, unlike Anil and Rina, the next couple I'll talk about. This was an extraordinary story the likes of which I'd never had before.

At first, the situation looked fairly standard. A wedding between two young people in their twenties, who adored each other. The groom, Anil, invited me out for a coffee to discuss it, so I duly accepted and trotted off to meet them a couple of days later.

However, instead of getting to meet Anil and his intended, the morning coffee turned into a very cloak-and-dagger affair with the young man and his cousin Essa.

They were very unclear about the circumstances to start with, but in the end, it transpired that Anil and his 'intended' Rina were from different castes, and the family would never have approved of them marrying.

I was puzzled. Surely I was here to discuss just that? If the family didn't approve, then how could we move things forward?

Anil looked sheepish for a moment. "Well to be honest, we already have," he explained. "We've actually been legally married, in secret, for over two years already."

I was aghast. "But the family doesn't know? At all?"

Anil confirmed this was the case. They still lived as part of their own families at home. They talked on disposable 'burner' phones that nobody knew about. And they met in secret, whenever they could (usually bolted on to visits to the cash-and-carry, as both families ran supermarkets).

"That's a lot of covering your tracks," I said. "You really couldn't just come clean?"

Both young men looked visibly horrified. "We'd be murdered for dishonouring our respective families," said Anil simply.

"But don't worry," said Essa. "We're tooled up. If anyone challenges us, we can defend ourselves." He then pulled back his jacket a little to show me, should I have doubted it, that he was carrying a machete. In a wine bar in Sutton Coldfield, at lunchtime!!

But even though I was shocked, and not a little scared, I just had to complete the scenario in my mind. How, I wondered, if the family didn't approve, could all of this happen?

"Things have moved on," explained the cousin, in shady verbal shorthand. "Debts have accrued. Some money has exchanged hands to, let's say 'help out' a failing business. Rina is part of the deal, Inshallah. So now, our two rival families are combining businesses rather than working against each other.

"An official 'match' has been approved. But it's really important that they don't know of Anil and Rina's history, as this will destroy everything. They have to be seen to be meeting for the first time in this capacity."

My head span. Not just at the concept of such a massive deception, but also as to how the caste issue had seemingly been erased by money.

Anil then took up the story. "And so that's where you come in Ruth. With your marriage service. Please will you marry us and make it look real?"

This felt like an enormous responsibility. As previously explained, the services we provide are, to all intents and purposes, the 'real' wedding day. But we can't do the legals for people, and that was obviously what he was wanting.

It would be dishonest to pretend that we could. I told him the best I could do was offer a 'Celebration Of Marriage' certificate, in fancy writing and all.

"And you sign it at the front of the room, so everyone will be able to see you doing it," I added hopefully.

"But people will want to see it up close," he added miserably. "Can you just change the wording a little?"

I said I was sorry, but no. By then I couldn't wait to leave, it all felt very dark and threatening. And I felt genuinely sad for a couple that had got themselves into such a mess that they feared for their lives. We work miracles daily, but that was probably one step too far.

Equally awful but for different reasons was the outdoor vow renewal in Staffordshire where the wind was so brutal it tore a page straight out of my folder.

Everyone watched, clinging on to their hats and shawls as the piece of paper danced off into the next field. I was so shocked I temporarily forgot the bride's name!

But the mercurial mistrals weren't done with us yet! After this, the wind still had enough energy to whip up the backdrop (some slash-glitter curtains like you'd have found in a 1980s working men's club) to such an extent that it whacked us all simultaneously in the face. The bride reeled back, tripped on her train and knocked over the vials that were waiting for the sand ceremony to round it all off. To say it was a disaster was an understatement.

In direct contrast from a service that was barely completed, we've the story from a colleague about a couple who seemingly couldn't marry enough times. On our Facebook forum she wrote:

'Just arrived to do a wedding ceremony. The couple got married in Vegas just the two of them. So this second service is especially for the groom's mum, as she was not happy.

'Sadly, she's now broken down on the way to the service and won't be here for at least three hours. The couple only have the ceremony venue for another two hours so I will have to do it twice. Once here as arranged, and again at the reception venue when the groom's parents arrive.

I think they will be well and truly married after all three!'

A friend of mine has a whole raft of wedding stories gleaned from her time working as a top-flight event planner. Davina's clients are incredibly wealthy and demand nothing but the best. The weddings take place in exotic locations and depending on the budget her role can cover every aspect from organising travel for every single guest; dressing the venue and recruiting and managing her teams of staff, right up to surfing the internet for bridal knickers at four in the morning.

Davina's clients treat her somewhere between a bonded slave and their new best friend, on-call every minute of the day, but of course she charges handsomely for it. That's not something we celebrants can get away with (it's more of a vocational role in truth), but then again, nobody's asking me to source their knickers for them.

What Davina did object to recently though (I'll keep the details vague here for obvious reasons), was being screamed at by a bride for not putting sun cream on her triplets during the Italian midday heat.

Davina responded that she wasn't the nanny, which wasn't received well, and apparently it went downhill from there.

"Honestly Ruth," she said when she got home and regaled me with the story, "I'd had a gut full of it. The bride had already tried to charge me ten euros for a burger at the staff table, which I hadn't had time to eat. Before that she'd accused me of pinching her Rolex, which one of the kids turned out to be carrying around with them, so I really wasn't feeling the love by then.

"Maybe she'd have been a bit more grateful if she'd known what I was doing all morning to keep her safe."

"What do you mean?" I asked, full of curiosity.

"We'd had a terrorist threat," Davina replied. "A high-profile mixed-race couple of reality tv stars. One of them had said something deemed to be anti-Muslim a few years back, and it obviously hadn't been forgotten.

"We got a threat the day before the wedding. We're in bloody

Sardinia by then. We had to get the police involved, which led to international police coming on board. By the end of it there was an SAS team patrolling the bay; you just couldn't make it up. There's me pulling my hair out, worried sick that everyone might be shot or blown to bits, and she's telling me off for not putting cream on the kids!"

I honestly don't know how Davina does it, but that's the thing; funerals and weddings truly do bring out the best and the worst in people. She also had a case where a bride's father had a heart attack just after the ceremony. Incredibly, the woman was seen leaning over her father as he was being stretchered away, screaming about how she'd never forgive him for ruining her big day!

I remember every single one of my wedding couples. Partly because I've done far fewer weddings and partly because the services are so unique. Each one contains an element or a moment that stays with me so of course they are, for the most part, very happy memories. The only couple that didn't fit into that category were Abbey and Joe.

This charmless pair booked me as their celebrant around a year in advance, and despite repeated requests, they never had the time to meet for a chat. I offered to travel to Oxford (about seventy miles away), but they were always too busy.

I then followed my back-up format: an initial questionnaire to get to know them, both as individuals and a couple. This would glean some information on where they'd met, how they got together and the progress of the relationship.

Other things to know were also what they wanted to include in the service in terms of content and other people. The venue was a lovely country house in Oxfordshire that didn't have a licence for weddings, so we had carte blanche as to what we could do.

I asked them in detail things like; were they writing love letters at all and if so, would they be in secret? Was she being 'given away'? Would they walk down the aisle together or Abbey on her own? Were both sets of parents alive, and if so, would they have any input? How about music – would it be live or recorded?

There's always so much to know in order to plan it properly, and it's such an important day, why wouldn't anyone give it their time and energy?

I think it was around one month before the wedding, and I'd had no information from them. I was panicking slightly, as this is also the time I'd normally be sending the final script for approval, and asking for the remainder of my fee. They'd given me a £100 deposit, but that was all, and I was feeling decidedly insecure about the whole thing by then.

Eventually, I did get some information from them, but it was like wringing blood out of a stone. There was no communication and definitely no warmth, and with just rings and vows specified, the service seemed very basic. There was no music, and nobody else involved. I began to wonder why, if they didn't want personalisation and warmth, they'd chosen a celebrant at all?

On the actual day, pitiful script in hand, I turned up in plenty of time. However, I've never experienced anything like what happened next. Everyone was gathered in the marquee in the grounds, sweltering in the heat, when the best man came forwards to whisper that the bride was running two hours late. I made an announcement from the front of the venue, at which everyone let out a collective groan, got out of their chairs and made for the door.

The guests then hung around outside in small, furtive clusters, smoking, chatting and looking generally hacked-off. I stood to the side by the drinks table, uncomfortable in my high shoes and formal suit, not sure what to do, silently furious at how things were unfolding.

I was sipping on lemonade when I got into conversation with someone, who chatted for all of two minutes before informing me that the bride was a 'total bitch'.

That took me aback somewhat. I'd pretty much got that impression from our interaction so far, but obviously, I was there in a professional capacity, so I wasn't going to agree. However, I didn't need to, her 'friend' did all the talking.

She told me all about the bride's ex boyfriends ('he was the one who used to sniff cocaine off her tits'), and then I heard all about what a gold-digger Abbey was, ending with, "You've seen that wart on the end of Joe's nose? Funny how him being a stockbroker makes it fade away. Eh?!"

I was just processing this, when the bride's sister appeared. She had a cigarette dangling and a glass of Prosecco in hand. "What a fiasco," she screeched. "Typical of Abbey. Selfish cow. Don't know how you've coped with her!"

I mumbled something about being used to long-distance planning, but the sister wasn't listening. She was keen to get the next barb in.

"Yeah. Probably having a hissy fit over something. I didn't even want to be here, but mum said she'd dis-inherit me if I didn't. So here I am. Happy bloody wedding day!" She raised the glass to no-one in particular, and tottered off back to her gang.

Abbey eventually arrived, but not before several others had shared their opinions with me. Unusually, some of them were also men. We all know women can be bitchy, but it's unusual to find criticism from both sexes, and from both the bride and the groom's side.

I have to say, it was a little unfair. Not because Abbey wasn't a bitch (she most certainly turned out to be); but because nothing was levelled at Joe, who seemed equally unpleasant.

There was little warmth between the couple, hardly any eye contact, and without doubt, it was the most disappointing service I've ever done. The only time they seemed anywhere near close, was when I stumbled over a word, and they simultaneously burst out laughing at my mistake.

After the service, I discreetly approached Joe for the remainder of the fee. Abbey was standing close by, and shot over to her husband's side.

"Payment? We've already done that!"

I pointed out I'd only had a deposit. At this point, Joe chipped in, "Well. You're going to have to wait. We're in a stately home. What are you going to do… march us to a cashpoint?" He brayed loudly, amused at his own patronising idea of wit.

I took a deep breath, forcing myself to keep calm, informing them in a very firm way that I'd call first thing in the morning. Honeymoon or not, I'd give them my bank details to do a bank transfer.

I later spoke to the venue manager who was incensed on my behalf, declaring them 'royal pains in the arse.'

He then pulled out the trump card, saying, "But don't worry darling. I've got their credit card details on file. I'll put it through as an excess payment and get you the money if they don't cough up."

That made me feel a tad better about the fiasco, but I couldn't wait to get home. It had been a long gruelling day, the culmination of a long gruelling 'relationship' with Abbey and Joe, and one that I couldn't wait to sever.

As I was packing the car, the band arrived for the evening. By amazing coincidence, I saw it was one of my friends, Simon. Abbey and Joe had plumped for his band 'Central Park' ('All Your Favourite Dancefloor Fillers – All Night!')

I asked him later on the phone, how the evening had gone? Simon responded that he too had enjoyed a 'first'. For me, it had been the guests coming outside to slag off the bride. And for him, it had been the sight of the bride dancing towards her guests, and every one of them, very subtly, turning their backs and dancing away from her.

This is such a shame, as that young woman will one day be old. One day she'll die. And then the celebrant will have to go to their 'Not Close To Family So Not Much To Say' file, and find the words to fill that thirty minute slot.

Wouldn't it be much better to live kindly and with generosity? To leave a real legacy of something worthwhile. This is summed up beautifully the following reading I sometimes turn to:

The Train Of Life (by Marv Hardin)

Life is like a journey on a train, with its stations,
with changes of routes and accidents.

We board this train when we are born,
and our parents are the ones who got our ticket.

We believe they will always travel on this train with us.

However at some station, our parents will get off the train
leaving us alone on this journey.

As time goes by other passengers will board the train,
many of whom will be significant;
our siblings, friends, children and even the love of our life.

Many will get off during the journey
and leave a permanent vacuum in our lives.

Many will go unnoticed:
we won't even know when they vacate their seats and get off the train.

This train ride will be full of joy, sorrow, expectations,
hellos, goodbyes and farewells.

A good journey is helping, loving and having a
good relationship with all co-passengers making
sure that we give our best to make the
journey comfortable.

The mystery of this fabulous journey is we do not know
at which station we ourselves are going to get off,
so we must live in the best way, adjust, forgive
and offer the best of what we have to give.

It’s important to do this because when the time comes for us
to leave our seat we should leave behind beautiful memories
for those who will continue their journey.

Thank you all for being co-passengers with dear Abbey on her journey through life.

CHAPTER 7: THE THINGS WE DO FOR LOVE

Most of the couples I deal with are younger and starting out together for the first time. But there's still a fair portion of older couples who have found love again after a divorce or the death of a spouse. These are the ones I learn from.

Through hearing the most incredible stories of courage, fate, chance and timing I've seen the power of hope; that things will always change if you give it long enough.

I've learnt about perseverance; that if you give up and don't keep trying, love won't find you. If you want it enough you have to keep on believing that it's out there somewhere, waiting for you nearby.

I've realised that love shouldn't hurt. Nobody has the right to own or control you. Butterflies in the stomach and living on one's nerves is not love. There's a fantastic passage from the book Captain Corelli's Mandolin that sums it up:

'Love is a temporary madness,
it erupts like volcanoes and then subsides.
And when it subsides you have to make a decision.
You have to work out whether your roots have so entwined together
that it is inconceivable that you should ever part.
Because this is what love is.
Love is not breathlessness,
it is not excitement,
it is not the promulgation of eternal passion.

That is just being "in love" which any fool can do.
Love itself is what is left over when being in love has burned away,
and this is both an art and a fortunate accident.
Those that truly love,
have roots that grow towards each other underground,
and when all the pretty blossom have fallen from their branches,
they find that they are one tree; and not two'

This also helped me fifty-eight years in, to be realistic. To understand that nobody is perfect but if you share common values; respect each other; share laughter and tears openly, and just know this is your person for life, then who could ask for more?

I saw a perfect example of this when I married Mo and Lula in her grandma's bedroom at home. Grandma had been given just a couple of weeks to live, so the two of them desperately wanted her to see them tie the knot. She was too ill to get up, so they figured why not take the wedding to her?

I'd done a bedside wedding before for a couple who were terminally ill, but never for a couple with an ill guest in attendance. However, not only was it beautiful, it was probably one of the most moving, intimate experiences I'd ever had.

With just six people in attendance, we stood against a home-made flower wall, erected to give the room a focal point and a bit of colour. The rest of the colour was provided by the guests. Mo's parents were in ceremonial traditional African clothing, and Lula's mum and dad in traditional but bright conventional wedding clothing. Even grandma had a brand new bed jacket on, all ribbons and bows. Rather incongruously they'd found her a fascinator to wear too.

Decorated with feathers and baubles, poor gran didn't seem very thrilled with her headwear. I lost count of the times I saw her tugging at it, looking uncomfortable or cross, muttering 'Get these curlers out'. But we'll ignore that because it's not the main thrust of the story.

When everyone was settled, I welcomed in the bride and did a little scene-setting, before continuing: "So many people believe a wedding has to be huge, noisy, expensive and in full public view, to be authentic. But this small, intimate gathering, in Nan's chapel of love means so much more.

"There are no acquaintances to impress. This is far more real – an intimate service, performed in a room full of love, before family, and in the eyes of God."

We then continued with some readings, and then the vows and rings, followed by the signing of a certificate; all viewed on Zoom by the bride's brother in Australia.

Throughout it all I couldn't take my eyes off the bride's grandfather, the way he held his wife in her bed, supporting her head so she could see. Whispering quietly to comfort her in her confusion, obviously still loving this lady dearly after sixty five years of marriage.

We'd had a little chance to chat in the garden beforehand. Their home was humble to say the least; despite working hard neither of them had earned much during their lifetime.

"But that doesn't matter Ruth," he said. "It's family that counts. You can have all the money in the world and still be lonely. Nobody in this family will go into care. Nobody will eat Sunday lunch on their own; or die alone. We've only got the basics materially but my God we're rich people in love and support. Nothing else matters."

All of that was going through my head as I drew the service to a close, still transfixed by this elderly couple who would be bound together until she took her last breath.

What does it take to find that kind of love, I wondered?

With that in mind, I did a little research about what makes a good relationship, and amongst all the dross and filler articles, I found a really in-depth and considered piece based on the advice of 1,500 long-term couples.

What really stood out, was the frequency of the same advice – the researcher commented how the same things cropped up over and over again, so seeing as we're in a section about marriage, I'd like to share it with you. Who knows, if you're considering the 'M' word, or going through a bad patch, it may help.

1. Be Together For The Right Reasons:
Not for looks, or money or peer pressure. Not because you're lonely or broke. Quite simply, be with someone because that person makes you happy and you love being with them.

2. Have Realistic Expectations
A love that's alive is constantly evolving. It expands and contracts. It deepens and mellows. It's not going to always be the way it was and it won't look the same in a year or two years' time.

Understand that some days you'll wake up and think, 'Oh no – you're still here?' But also understand that feeling is normal. And that sticking things out is worth it, because that too will change. In a day, or perhaps next week, or in six weeks, you'll look again at that person and a giant wave of love will wash over you. You'll love them so much you think your heart is going to burst. Understand this dynamic, and there'll be no rush for divorce at the first sign of problems.

3. Respect is Key
Your love will wax and wane. Your communication will be better sometimes than others. But what can't recover, is loss of respect. Always act honourably and decently towards each other. Be the best you can be – the hardest working, and the kindest.

Good people foster good feelings towards each other. Respect each other's individuality and absolutely do not badmouth each other in private. This will erode respect quicker than anything.

4. Talk Openly About Everything
And that includes the painful things. Honesty, openness and transparency are key. Tackle the difficult things when times are good.

5. A Healthy Relationship Requires TWO healthy individuals
Co-dependency is not healthy. Each person must maintain their own identity, their own interests and their own perspective. Attempting to coerce or control your partner is not love. Having to change to suit someone is not healthy, or sustainable.

6. Give Each Other Space
Whether that's separate bank accounts, credit cards, friends, hobbies, vacations, bathrooms or bedrooms. Insecurity is not a reason to stop someone having their own life too.

7. Change Is Inevitable – Accept It.
One contributor commented that at her wedding, an elderly family member told her, "One day many years from now, you will wake up and your spouse will be a different person: make sure you fall in love with that person too."

We're talking about really deep changes here – perhaps changing religions; moving countries; dealing with the death of family members (including children); supporting elderly family members; changing political beliefs; even changing sexual orientation or gender identification. It's unrealistic to expect life to stay the same.

8. Learn How To Deal With Conflict.
Name calling, stonewalling, contempt and defensiveness do not solve issues. Neither does dragging old issues into a new one.

Talking and negotiation are better. Taking a breather always helps.

And remembering why you got together in the first place. List ten reasons why you fell for your partner. This is hugely helpful in re-establishing balance and perspective.

And finally – when someone wins, there's always a loser. Always aim for a draw.

9. Learn To Forgive.
Most things are actually not worth getting upset over. Let it go.

10. Don't Make Kids The Complete Focus
You made them. You are all individuals, and whilst they will consume your life for a certain time, don't make this the only way. Love produced them, and they will need to see that love around them, in order to grow into healthy adults.

11. Create Relationship Rules
Ways to live by that help you stay harmonious. Things that are important to you, to each other. If one of you works in an office all day, and the other works from home, then it makes sense for the home-worker to get the washing done whilst they are there.

The same for finances – how much debt are you both happy with? Vacations – will they be together or apart? The list goes on, but just as in any democratic society, there has to be an agreed way of living, of co-existing to make the wheels turn smoothly.

12. Sex Matters!
Sex keeps a relationship healthy, and heals an ailing one. When things break down, sex is the first casualty. Schedule in time for sex (whether you feel like it or not) – it's a reset button that has amazing benefits.

13. The Little Things Add Up
Don't stop doing the small things in your relationship. Cumulatively, they mean a lot.

That means giving compliments, noticing your partner and acknowledging them. Sending flowers, leaving notes and being good at buying gifts.

Love and adore each other. Work together as a team. Nurture yourselves and your environment. Be grateful for what you have.

Discuss problems sooner rather than later, and go to counselling before you really need it, if you need it.

I could see from that list several areas where things had fallen short over the years. Either in my own behaviour, my expectations or even my lack of expectations. But now armed with such sage advice, I felt confident that my new relationship would go from strength to strength.

This belief was shored up later on down the line when Russ and I were reviewing the week over a glass of wine.

He confided in me how people at work had said he'd changed. There was no huge discussion about this apparently; it wasn't a negative observation, but they'd noted he was a snappier dresser these days; that he was more outgoing, and also that his sense of humour had returned.

In addition to the physical changes (he'd let his lovely wavy grey hair come through and also grown a goatee), I guess people couldn't help but see a different man.

"Is it Ruth?" someone had questioned. "It's all her doing isn't it?"

Russ told me how that had both caught him off guard and made him laugh. It had made him think too.

"So what did you tell them?"

"Not too much," was the reply. "I said you'd given the thumbs up to the changes, but it wasn't you that suggested them."

He paused to swig some wine before continuing.

"But what I didn't tell them is how you've given me the confidence to change. Actually, the inspiration to change. You make me want to be a better person. I'm interested in life again. I can see a future now the boys are growing up, and it's bright.

"I feel guilty for admitting it Ruth. But I've come to realise that through losing one person, I found two more. You and myself."

CHAPTER 8: THE SEARCH FOR BALANCE

With words like that, I'd begun to feel secure for the first time probably ever. Finally able to be myself. It meant letting him see me with no make-up, and being confident that it was okay not to have my hair immaculate every minute of the day. The un-polished imperfect me seemed more than good enough. And it was *such* a relief.

But it wasn't all plain sailing. To say I was struggling with the limitations of children would be an under-statement. Here we were approaching the time we should have been able to take it easy, and there were two teenagers, with their bubbling hormones, needs and wants, to now consider.

I hated my selfishness, for wanting things my way. And I hated my partner's consistent softness for giving in when they wanted things their way. I got angry when Aaron came in late and crashed and bashed around the house, waking everyone up. I got mildly depressed at the lack of conversation and how everyone seemed happy to be around the breakfast table with a phone.

"It's just their relaxation time," explained Russ.

"But it's bloody rude," I said. "Headphones on means nobody's even trying to talk. Why aren't you asking about their day and what they've got planned? If they're in for dinner or not? Anything, but I can't stand the silence."

Once that had been taken on board, I then tried to instigate the idea of a Saturday job. The kids looked at me as if I'd suggested we barbeque the dog.

"It'll do you good," I insisted. "Your social skills will get better; new doors will open; you never know who you're going to meet!"

The headphones went back on and the meal ended as it had begun.

I remember that and other mornings like it, would generally lead on to not so good days. Days where we'd bicker gently and then not so gently about the boys. They were his kids, but I genuinely felt with my breadth of experience I could help them grow up, if only he'd let me.

On bad days I'd wonder if we could survive, or at least how we'd ever move forward. It turned out Russ had been having the same thoughts. Every now and then he'd ambush me with a 'Where do you think we're going in this relationship?' kind of chat. But no matter how bad the moments were, we always managed to pull it back in a civil, loving way.

"It's just that I can't bear to lose you," he admitted eventually. "If you are going anywhere, then I need to know. It'll kill me, but if you can't deal with us as a package, then you have to say."

I understood what he meant. That the parental bond is unbreakable. This is the man who'd stumbled upon the kids as eight year olds, watching them pour 7-UP down the toilet to see if it dissolved the poo or exploded it. This is the man who spent all day at work dying to get home so his toddlers could rush up to him and cling to his legs and say they'd missed him. That stuff doesn't just go away, it's a lifelong commitment.

I thought how ironic it was, that I'd had all the freedom in the world and it hadn't made me happy. And now, although I had the opposite of what I thought I needed, in reality it had brought me what I'd been seeking. I realised then I needed to stop wishing them away and relax into becoming part of the team instead.

"They'll grow up," Russ promised. "They'll be off to university soon, and then it'll be work, and you'll be sick of all the time you have to spend with me! You'll be taking on more services than ever just to get away!"

I remember laughing at that, thinking 'Never!' Russ was just too lovely to not want to be around. And besides, work was getting a tad more dangerous as time went on, I'd much prefer to be spending time at home with him instead.

Other colleagues agree on this too, that people's attitudes have definitely changed and the potential for aggression is much more part of the daily scene. This was evidenced by the case of Mabel McCracken, the Irish matriarch with a surprising number of burly sons in prison.

Mabel's funeral story is an interesting one, as normally our work would be classed as white collar, performed in a safe environment. Her case proved that actually, the job is not without its surprises and risks.

It started at the family meeting. Set against the backdrop of a very tough Birmingham housing estate, I remember just two of her daughters being present, along with their immediate families.

They'd been polite but terse, giving minimal information, supplemented by a few scraps of paper from the brothers including one called Derek. His scribbles described how she'd been 'a great mam,' and that he'd never forget her. There wasn't enough to fill five minutes of a service let alone half an hour, so again, I did my usual digging underneath the surface story, as there is generally more to say when people feel encouraged.

As an aside, I have to mention that sometimes this softly-softly approach can work too well, unleashing a torrent of information that is, let's say, inappropriate, or possibly un-usable. Like the time a colleague asked someone if their son had produced any children.

"Oh no," volunteered his mother happily, "He had a very small penis so it wasn't possible you see."

We're always ready for the unexpected, which is probably a good job, but on this occasion, my probing and asking questions about Mabel in an alternative way just produced some standard, if slightly more expansive information.

As the daughters talked I began to see a picture of a strong lady – one who'd worked hard as a cleaner; someone who had always been there emotionally for her kids, and pretty much raised them as a single mother after her husband disappeared off with another woman.

She'd made thick hearty stews from scrag ends of meat; and knitted garments for them all, which were passed down according to age.

And then, when the youngest had finally outgrown their sweaters and cardigans, the garment would be unpicked, the wool re-wound and knitted into something else.

This amazing lady re-cycled before it had been heard of. She re-purposed everything; nothing had gone to waste. But although there was obvious poverty, most importantly, everyone knew they'd been loved.

She also had humour; this was demonstrated by the legendary family story of how the youngest had gone into the front parlour to tell his mum the others were picking on him, saying he'd been a 'mistake'. Without a beat, Mabel had apparently said, "Go back in there and tell them they were all mistakes!"

Sadly this was the only humorous bit of content. There was nothing else to really balance Mabel's story out. No happy holidays; no loving relationship after being left. No tales of nights out with the girls, or interesting hobbies to be mentioned. It was another of those services where I needed to focus on love and the importance of family.

In cases like this, I usually announce to the mourners that 'Although the service will be short, it will concentrate on the right things. Because, when we gather to remember someone, it's not the material goods we recall but rather, who someone has been to us.' And then I continue on with the words mentioned earlier, about how someone has behaved towards us; their spiritual legacy, if you like.

This is summed up perfectly by a quote from American Author Neil Strauss:

'What if people thought about their life not in terms of what they've accomplished or accumulated or experienced, but in terms of the effect they've had on others?'

Those words really touched me, fitting perfectly into the scenario of Mabel's life. So, alongside my introduction, and closing words and some lovely readings, the service eventually shaped up nicely.

I was therefore feeling more confident of doing a good job for the family right up until I arrived at the crem and saw the car park was full of men in dark suits, sitting in even darker cars.

There was also a police dog and its handler by the entrance and hordes of agitated people gathered outside. They were engulfed in clouds of smoke, and I heard dark mutterings about 'The Fuzz' as I passed.

"What's all this Andy?" I said to the chapel attendant. "Something feels really wrong."

Andy laughed in amusement. "Don't you know you're doing a gangland funeral?"

I was more than taken aback that the FD hadn't thought to mention it in advance. A hugely important detail given the chances of things kicking off.

"Ah don't worry," Andy continued, laughing now. "You'll be fine in this bit. It's the graveside part where you need to worry."

(Just to explain at this point. Most services are conducted entirely inside the crematorium. This one was a slightly more unusual 'split' service, with the main part inside, and then the committal at the graveside, followed by the burial).

"So what, exactly is the issue with that bit?" I asked.

"The family want to do the back-filling themselves," Andy replied, making a shovelling action as he did so.

I was still none-the-wiser. I couldn't see a problem with everyone working together to fill the grave as a family.

Andy sighed as if I was the most stupid organism on the planet.

"Think about it," he said, tapping the side of his head as he spoke. "They're gangsters. Two rival families outside. One's come to pay their respects, and the other family are here to make sure the old bird's gone. If it's gonna kick off anywhere it'll be at the graveside because they'll all have spades! Weapons. Capiche?!"

So with that charming thought planted in my mind, I spent the next fifteen minutes talking about love, whilst watching a perfect demonstration of the opposite unfolding before me.

Derek, one of the absent sons (who looked strangely familiar but I couldn't think why), was there at the back, handcuffed to his prison officer. The daughters were at the other side of the crem, not speaking or looking in his direction.

The place was an absolute cauldron of tension, so I was really surprised when the prison officer un-cuffed Derek to allow him to pay his respects to his mum, by coming up and placing a rose on her coffin.

That bit went well, but on the way back to his officer, Derek took the opportunity to literally swipe at someone as he passed them by.

And that was it – we were off. A mass brawl ensued. Flowers sailed through the air, and the fists flew. A broken bottle appeared from nowhere and a pew had been upturned by the time the officers from the car park burst through the doors.

It took another twenty minutes to clear the chapel and remove the offenders, by which time Derek's guard was probably contemplating his demotion or sacking. Either way, he and Derek had disappeared, along with all the brawlers.

Only the two sisters and their families remained. We made our way in silence to the graveside, to continue the service.

I was determined to give Mabel the last bit of the send-off she deserved, but it all felt a bit flat, and very sad by the time I'd done.

I closed on my usual words, 'And so I'll leave you now with your thoughts and those dearest to you;' and having waved them goodbye, I gently picked my back way across the graveyard.

And as I did so, I pondered on the irony of meeting up with Derek again.

Although he hadn't recognised me, I'd placed him in my mind. I'd taught him English in a young offenders' unit probably a decade or so beforehand. One of the many, many jobs along the way, this role had been more about fire-fighting than getting any real language into the lads, their vocabularies were so poor it really was a lost cause.

I cringe now, looking back at how I'd even tried to teach them about collective nouns. Trying to explain how it was a descriptive way of listing groups of the same things. "For example," I'd said, "Think of a wise old owl. That's why we say a 'parliament' of owls, because they look clever.

"And the same for crows," I continued. "They look threatening, so we'd say a murder of crows."

I then asked for examples of what they knew already. Up came the usual suspects; a school of dolphins, a flock of birds etc.

"I know miss," someone then piped up. "How about a rack of lamb?"

I couldn't blame him, although I did laugh uproariously in the staff toilets later on. These guys had endured difficult starts in life; they survived on small vocabularies and big plans, of leading gangs and heading up families of crime.

But the one thing I did manage to get them all to do in my time at the unit, was to write a short essay about the people they loved most.

Derek had written about his mum. With his limited grasp of language, he'd managed to tell the story of a woman who'd held down four jobs to keep her kids. He'd been illegitimate and Mabel could have chosen to have him adopted, but she hadn't.

She'd even donated a kidney to her son along the way, prompting me to think, if ever there was a demonstration of love, surely that had to be it?

So why wasn't any of this in the service?

The answer, as mentioned previously, was the privilege of being the chief mourner; first come, first served. There's no way Derek or any of his brothers in prison would have had an opportunity to get this information to me as they weren't the people in charge of the event. The sisters had enjoyed the final say, and there was nothing anybody could have done about it. No wonder tensions erupted on the day.

Happily, violence and bad behaviour aren't the normal modus operandi, but I guess the more funerals one does, the greater the chance of encountering extraordinary circumstances.

I was chatting to someone who works outside my area at a different crem, who agrees whole-heartedly. Based in the very heavily multi-cultural area of Handsworth there are pockets where it's very gang-orientated.

This man had a gun pulled on him during lockdown, when he attempted to control the amount of people wanting to attend a service. He was also there when an armed gang broke into the office, tied up the three staff and raided over £5k from the safe.

Not content with that, these poor people were then taken hostage and driven in the back of a van, whilst the rest of the gang stole a JCB digger from the cemetery, intending to smash through the rear wall of a nearby bank.

The hostages were then thrown out of the van as a distraction, whilst the gang made off with £21k in stolen money! Caught by the police minutes later, it ended with the gang running for their freedom, scattering guns and money everywhere as they went.

Honestly, people have no idea of what goes on behind the scenes. And thinking about it, that's probably for the best!

CHAPTER 9: WHEN FUNERALS GO WRONG

The vast majority of times most services go well, but Mabel's was a perfect example of when they don't. That's inevitable I guess as we're dealing with uncontrollable elements, from the weather through to people.

Sometimes the problems are tiny things that fit under the category of 'What Not To Say At The Crematorium Door,' like the lady who may possibly have had a little drink, who shouted out to the bearers 'Don't drop him now will you!'

I had to diffuse that one very quickly with a jaunty "Oh Mary, you are naughty! You're the only person who's ever actually said that!"

Another random yelling out was from a child with her mother. They'd obviously been to the service before mine. The little girl skipped past and very loudly exclaimed, "Oh look mummy. There's another one!"

An audible groan of horror went up from the crowd.

Kenny is also a guilty party in this section. He once appeared at the front door to do his coffin plate reading, just as everyone was taking up their places outside.

The end of his loud conversation with someone in the foyer coincided with a hush falling over the crowd, so everyone heard; "Ooh, I'm in ever such a good mood. Birmingham won three nil last night!"

This segued seamlessly into "Yes, you're alright mate. Crack on," as he checked the plate, oblivious to the daggers he was getting from the crowd.

Then we move on to things not to do and say once inside the crematorium like when my friend invited people on a very chilly day to "Come inside everyone; it's a lot warmer in here."

The response was, "Yes, I guess it would be."

Discreetly dotted all around the crem there are now notices reminding us to behave as if we were always on camera. Live-streaming the service to viewers all over the world never used to happen before Covid, but now it's hugely popular.

Several videographers have caught on to the fact that it's a lot easier to turn up at the crem and stream a service rather than all the fuss of a wedding, so yes, we do have to be mindful that things may be 'live' on the day.

However, before this was commonplace, I was caught out more than once pulling up my tights or faffing with an errant bra strap, with no clue people were tuning in from all over the world for such a special preview!

Another example is from a service a friend attended, where a vicar was performing a second time for a family. Apparently he said:

"Well sadly, this is a return visit. It was just a year ago I stood here doing Clive's service, and now it's his brother Bill. They were very different characters; Clive was a devout Christian, so we know where he's gone. But Bill? I'm not quite so sure about him ..."

There are other memories for me too. Just small things that stick in the mind, like the service I did where a child of about six years old sat at the front, loudly munching and rustling a bag of crisps for the entire thirty minutes.

Or the celebration of life for a lady who was all about family and believed in children expressing themselves without rules or discipline. This played out exactly as threatened, when her four-year-old granddaughter was allowed to 'free range' around the crem, shouting, throwing herself on the floor and generally behaving badly. When she climbed up onto the raised platform beside me though I did think surely someone, anyone, would call her back?

But no! The family looked on as if it was all perfectly normal as little Amaryllis hung off one of my legs like she was preparing to pole dance.

I went a little off script then, joking "Ooh, we must have one of those treasured grandchildren up here. We can see why Eileen adored them all so much."

Turning to Amaryllis I then said, "Would you like to go back and sit with grandad sweetheart?"

She cast me a glance. A calculated devil look that only a stubborn, spoilt, slightly evil child can manage. Then she simply lifted up my skirt, semi-stuck her head under it and said "Eeeeuw!" in a disgusted voice.

That's when her mother finally came over and picked her up. Not a word of apology. How can anyone think that behaviour is okay?

Surprisingly, I managed to continue reading the script and not trip up, but nobody has 100% perfect track record in this department, ever.

A few slip-of-the tongue moments were discussed on our forum recently:

Celebrant 1: 'I had a bad day today. I invited a lady called Susan to come up and share her mammaries.'

Celebrant 2: 'Don't worry! We all have them. Whilst recounting The Gaelic Blessing from John Rutter today I nearly said 'Deep Heat' instead of 'Deep Peace.'

Celebrant 3: 'Yep! Mine today was during Psalm 23 (The Lord Is My Shepherd), when I said, 'He prepareth a table for me in the presence of my enemas."

Celebrants 1 & 2: "You win!"

Another never-to-be erased memory of mine happened at a crem miles away from me, where one thing after another went wrong. Some days are just like that, although thankfully they are very rare.

This is the one where a service ran so far over the timeslot that we may all just as well have got out our sleeping bags and camping stoves and settled in for the night.

To explain: I was acting in the role of mentor for a newly-qualified celebrant called Victoria. Being of no competition to me as she lived well outside of the area, I'd agreed to help her take the first fledgling steps into this unpredictable world of work.

The first job was to take her to the crem in advance of my service; show her the button that closes the curtains, and the ones that operate the music. I explained how the 'start music' button sometimes sticks a little but not to press it more than once, otherwise it skips to the next track. Victoria looked panicked even at that stage.

Afterwards, we had a little chat about how to work out service timings and as a final touch I introduced her to Kevin, the crem assistant on duty that day, who then took her on a tour behind the curtains.

Victoria said afterwards that she felt as prepared as she could be, without having met a family, which is lovely. But like I say, she hadn't seen the service yet.

Sadly, she didn't get the best of examples when the day came around. The first hitch was being taken on one side by Kevin to inform me that things were running a bit late, because the FD had forgotten the flowers, 'But not to worry 'cos one of the local ladies has stepped in.'

I asked what that meant, to be told they've a florist on standby for such occasions. Apparently, she always has a spare simple spray of flowers ready, and at the drop of a hat she jumps into the car, hurtles down the collector road, and meets the FD out the back of the public toilets.

Here, they place the flowers and then continue on their stately approach, past the toilets, along the tree-lined avenue, as if nothing has happened.

When we finally got in, I noticed how the chapel stunk really badly of fish and chips. Absolutely not acceptable of course, but explained by the fact that someone had left open the connecting door from the backrooms and office, to the public area.

I think the trouble here is that staff get so used to working in the environment, they forget that for others this is generally a solemn, heart-breaking occasion. People are in a building they'd rather not be in but if they have to be there, surely asking for everything to be in place, to be perfect, is a basic requirement?

We have so many senses, and so many ways of processing information, and if one of the components is out of kilter on such a vital day, it can really affect the overall experience. I'm not sure if I'd lost someone I'd have wanted to walk into chapel and have the smell of fish be the first thing that hit me.

But it was too late to seek out some air-freshener, the hearse had arrived and people would be seated within minutes.

When everyone was settled and had stopped fidgeting I did my usual welcoming words, and then invited up the first speaker, an eleven year old lovely little grandson who'd written a personal poem especially for 'Gandad.'

The problems started from the off. At first, he couldn't get his tablet to switch on. Then when he had, at first sight of his words this little chap just fell apart, sobbing all over the lectern, his poem completely incomprehensible.

Incredibly, nobody got up to help, so he blubbed on, eventually returning to his seat, having thrown the timings out by several minutes.

I then invited up the next speaker, who did a lovely job sharing her warm thought, and fabulous recollections. However, as she picked her A4 folder up off the lectern, she caught the button for the curtains; which then slowly began to close around her brother.

There was a scream from a section of the family seated at the front; they'd categorically requested that the curtains remained open. My heart plummeted, even as the mind went into overdrive.

Ideally, Kevin should have been there, but he was nowhere in sight. An FD would have been a good back up, but in reality they often just leave us to it and go outside to make their calls or have a cigarette. So this now meant I had to excuse myself (in the middle of a service!), with nothing happening and a load of upset people about to get angry.

It reminded me of my showbiz days in stand-up. In the early part of my career, when I was trying out different impressions, instruments and costume changes, one of the most useful bits of advice was, 'Never leave an empty stage. It's a sure-fire way to lose your audience.'

This was exactly what was about to happen now. So once I'd exited at a brisk but dignified pace, this changed to a sprint, as I sought out the elusive Kevin.

Incredibly, I found him in the car park sat in his truck, just preparing to leave on his part-time tat (scrap) round!

"Kevin," I screamed. "Get off your bloody truck will you. The curtains have closed early and I don't know where the 'open' button is. What the f*** are you doing?" I was frantic and furious, and he knew it.

"Oh balls," he responded, more irritated than urgent. "I thought the other bloke was back in the office. It only takes ten minutes to do a scattering, what's he doing I wonder?" Then, as an afterthought he added, "Shit! I'm gonna lose that washing machine now!"

Kevin leapt down from the truck, still grumbling, and dashed back to his office just inside the chapel. It's discreet, set at the back of the room with a glass window to oversee what's going on. And I then found out it houses the elusive button that re-opened the curtains and allowed me to continue on with the service. But not until I'd made him promise to stay the course; the scrap washing machine would have to wait.

Promise extracted, I then gathered my wits, and walked calmly back through the double doors. You could have heard a pin drop. And although it was the speaker who'd inadvertently closed the curtains, of course the overall responsibility for everything, would have been deemed to be mine.

I'm just glad the family didn't decide to sue, as per a documented case recently where £13k was paid out in damages, because a song was played out of order from the agreed listing!

Blimey, I thought; if this family had been so inclined, they'd have been millionaires. Especially as things continued to unfold in a similar vein during the reflection music.

As Glen Campbell's Rhinestone Cowboy played, I saw a few puzzled glances between the mourners. There's always an audible rustle, or some shuffling or whispering when something doesn't go right, and I could definitely detect the signs. But nobody was calling me over or looking directly at me, so I was clueless at that stage.

At the end of the service after the committal, final words and exit music I left the chapel. The chief mourner stomped over to me looking furious. The first words out of her mouth were, "The pictures were missing."

I was confused. "But there were photos on the coffin as requested?"

"No!" she snapped, "the ones to go with the music. The visual tribute up on the screen."

Kevin leapt straight in at that point, apologising profusely, already taking the lady's arm to steer her, and the entire crowd, back into the building.

"We can't have that," he said. "So sorry. Let's go back in and watch it now shall we?"

My heart almost scudded to a halt. He couldn't, could he? The next family's mourners were literally about to come in for their service. But no; on he ploughed, herding everyone through the doors. However, if I was horrified at the thought, it was nothing compared to what happened next.

Obviously, as we'd left, the guys behind the curtains had already removed the coffin. After a bit of frantic shouting that we were in fact on our way back in, the action began again as they pushed the coffin back through the hatch and onto the catafalque.

All I could hear from behind the curtains was a lot of scraping, some puffing and panting, and someone very loudly saying, "Fooking hell, he's heavy!"

We all sat through Rhinestone Cowboy once more. We watched pictures of the deceased as a little boy with his mum, then with his siblings and after that, at school.

Somewhere in-between Glen telling us how he'd been 'Walking these streets so long' and how he was 'Doin' a load of compromising' this handsome young buck turned into a careworn dad and suddenly an old man. Then he was gone. Just like that.

We shuffled out in silence; the family still not appeased and the next family waiting to come in, beyond angry that they'd been robbed of their time.

Victoria announced she'd 'have to think long and hard' about whether she could handle that kind of scenario.

And me? To this day, I still can't listen to Rhinestone Cowboy.

CHAPTER 10: AND RELAX!

It was the summer of 2021 that I started to feel the familiar signs of exhaustion. Having visited the doctors a couple of years previously I'd been advised my problem wasn't early-onset dementia as I'd feared.

Apparently putting my car keys in the trash (making me late for a service); and thinking it was Wednesday when it was Thursday (making me very late for a service) were all signs I was 'just' menopausal and overworked. As was putting the hot water bottle in the fridge; forgetting names and faces and not being able to recognise transactions on my credit card.

Now there were new symptoms to deal with: dodgy knees; lurking migraines and an almost ever-present brain fog. Was it age or something more sinister? Plainly there was a decision to be made. Take some time out for much-needed rest, but risk slipping off the radar? Or continue on doing five to eight services a week and risk slipping off this mortal coil?

My friend Tim offered some very sage, considered, eloquent advice.

"Fuck it," he said. "Life's too short. Take a break from it all. And besides," he added mischievously, "you're not that important. The world will still turn without you!"

Tim and I grew up across the street from each other. He was the first punk in our town of Sutton Coldfield, back in the days it was a 'nice' residential area. He'd stroll around in black eye liner and bondage trousers with straps so short he had to shuffle like an Egyptian.

Later on, I too was to break boundaries and become a tartan-clad

Bay City Roller-obsessed teen, and then a New-Romantic, complete with spiky hair, billowing silk trousers and shoulder pads you could land a helicopter on. We were odd but firm friends and stayed that way: we knew too much about each other to ever fall out.

I valued Tim's advice but as an extra back-up decided to consult the online forum that I belong to. People empathised with the dilemma and it was good to hear I wasn't the only one a) exhausted and b) operating from a poverty mentality.

Having grafted so hard to establish relationships with FDs and get work in the first place; and with so much competition (the market is completely saturated with celebrants) – it's a brave soul that takes time out. But the general consensus was to do it. And not to spend my time off tackling the housework, overdue accounts and all the other jobs that mount up, but rather to literally go off and have some real adventures.

It took a couple of months to process all this; to really consider that I may be jettisoning my career, but ultimately I took a deep breath and told all the FDs I work for that I was having a couple of months out. However, I was careful to let them know I *wasn't* retiring and *would* be back straight afterwards. Like a sort of maternity leave without the baby.

"Brilliant," said Tim. "Now you can have a break. Why don't you get a motorhome? I've done it for fifteen years and never regretted it. Think of the adventures ahead of you!"

Having visited the Camping and Motorhome Show earlier that year, it wasn't a hard sell. I'd spent the entire day there drooling at these £60k plus vehicles; exotic homes on wheels that promised king of the road type freedom, combined with adventure.

So yes, Tim's words, were all this impulsive Libran needed to find herself prowling the offerings at AEG Motorhomes in Stourbridge, albeit at the slightly less glamorous end of the forecourt.

"We've had this one back three times now," said the salesman Matt gleefully, as he guided me towards a less streamlined, older-looking model than most of the others. Bearing in mind my experience of internet dating when I've been overlooked for exactly those reasons, I decided to be open-minded.

After locating the keys we stepped inside this palace of promise, and I fell instantly in love. Entering through the rear door I saw a tiny kitchen, complete with fridge, cooker and storage/preparation area. Immediately next to this was the toilet and shower room, all done out in a once-jaunty but now slightly faded yellow. "It's a bit tired looking," I said.

"Well, she's eighteen years old," responded Matt, "but like I say we've had her in three times and tracked her from owner to owner. Look at the upholstery, it's immaculate. And we can guarantee the mileage as we've done the services every year. She's a nice little buy if you can stretch to it. Five berths too! Think of the adventures you and your friends could have."

In truth, I couldn't stretch to it. But like every other challenge in life, I wasn't going to be defeated. One more visit with an experienced motor-homer; a test drive around the ring road at Stourbridge; an excruciating hour or so arranging the finance, and she was mine!

Several things occurred to me on the terrifying journey home. The first was that I really did need to curb my impulsive streak; the one that has, in the past, seen me pop out to the shops to buy a sandwich and come home with a harp. The one that made me hack off all my long hair because I saw a style sported by supermodel Helena Christenson and thought it might suit me (it didn't). The one that saw me buy this motorhome with five years' debt attached to it, when I didn't even have a secure income stream.

The other thing to hit me was that I hadn't even measured the drive outside of my house; what a basic, schoolgirl error! It's a very steep incline and quite a narrow area in-between the garage and the front lawn; would the newly-named Myvanwy even fit?

This realisation ensured the last twenty minutes of the journey were tense, uncomfortable and full of regrets. These were temporarily assuaged when I got home and managed to edge her gingerly into place (I'd get used to the horrific scraping sound of the towbar as it dragged across the incline). Yes – Myvanwy was home and now we had to get to know each other before embarking upon our adventures.

The first week was painful. I couldn't remember a word Matt had said about what went where or what all the knobs and buttons were for. I couldn't get the electric heater on; nor work out the thermostat. The canopy didn't seem to want to unfurl; (it had sprung out magnificently in the showroom). So many things forgotten and so many things unknown. Did one travel with a full tank of water or was it best on an empty tank? How did I prevent the pipes from freezing on a frosty night in winter?

"Bloody hell" said Tim, eyes rolling in mock despair "did you listen to anything the salesman told you? The length of this list!" He looked tired just surveying it, but then he had come over straight from work; a day full of cutting lawns and trimming hedges. It was good of him to spare the time.

As a result of him doing so I finally understood a little better how to operate the vehicle and soon after, managed my first weekend away. After reversing into the safety post I'd had fitted on the drive, and flooding the water tank (yes, I'd plumped for the pre-fill option but not realised doing it on a slope was inadvisable), I was off. A solo trip to prove what a big girl I was. What could possibly go wrong?

Heading south from Birmingham down the M5, I'd decided to spend the first weekend at a campsite twenty miles away near Derbyshire with lovely walks and access to good local shops. Far enough for a 'proper' drive, yet near enough to come home should anything awful happen.

Reversing onto the hardstanding pitch when I got there was an interesting challenge (I nearly ran over the site warden and she wasn't best-pleased). But after we'd made peace, Kaz seemed happy enough to talk me through the control panel.

"This is for the electric heating. The outside dial is for on/off; and the inside dial is for temperature. You'll also need to switch on the system inside the wardrobe. Look – that button that says space heater. There's the one! Do you want to make notes as we go along?"

Ultimately I made pages and pages of notes, and it really helped. I put the kettle on and made a cup of tea; all good there. I opened the gas tanks in the side of the van and used the cooker; fantastic!

All was going beautifully until I got trapped in the shower room with the heating on full blast. Unable to get out, after about ten minutes it was positively stifling. My throat began to close up.

I shouted but nobody came. I lapped tepid water from the tap and tried again, with the same result. Determined I wasn't going to die alone, air-dried to a crisp in a motorhome toilet, I braced myself. Seconds later the door had been 'shouldered' down and was hanging by one hinge.

"Oh dear," said Kaz when she saw the damage, "that's not a great start."

"I know," I replied "but do you think you can help me re-hang it somehow? God, I wish I'd never started all this."

Kaz laughed at that comment. "Every single person who buys a caravan or motorhome; or even a boat for that matter, always says the same. There's a learning curve and it just all feels uphill. But once you know how to do everything it'll be second nature and then you'll enjoy her."

Those words stayed with me for a couple of months as the learning curve continued, but by the spring of 2022 I began to enjoy the van more. Short trips to National Trust properties; visits to sites around the country, and even a spot of 'wild camping' off grid.

One example was a winter weekend spent on a cliff top in the North Yorkshire fishing village of Staithes. Carved partly into and around the cliff itself, this picturesque hamlet was used as a film location for the Daniel Day-Lewis' film 'Phantom Thread'.

I found it enchanting, with its winding streets full of small galleries and coffee shops, local pubs and artisan bakers. All this was made so much more enjoyable knowing I could then return back to Myvanwy, perched on the clifftop car park, an alluring tin siren promising all the comforts of home.

It was on my second day that things began to feel less comfortable. Halfway through the afternoon, as I was catching up on some sleep, another motorhome arrived. It screeched noisily into the car park with music blaring. A third van arrived and soon after a fourth.

Peeping through the bedroom window I saw much activity. Despite it being chilly, out came camping tables and chairs. A fire-pit was produced from one van, and copious amounts of drink from another. Everyone settled down in their enormous coats and blankets for what was obviously going to be an ebullient 'meet' (camping terminology, for those who care).

I dared to venture out an hour or so later. There were lots of cheery hellos and how are yous? This was followed by some banter about where we all came from and what engine size our vans were. They asked if I was alone and I told them apart from my little terrier Gloria, I was.

"Well," said Rob from Halifax, "apologies in advance if things get a little noisy later. We do like a party us lot."

The entire group hooted as if Rob had told the funniest joke in the world. I then left them to it, bantering and drinking. I could hear Rob's partner Denise cackling even as I descended down the steep slope into the centre of Staithes.

As I walked, half of me wondered if I should just pack up and leave, I hadn't driven this far to have my solitude disturbed; but the other part of me argued I'd only just got there. "Besides, don't be snobbish Ruth," I said to myself, "Everyone's entitled to have fun."

I decided the best plan was to buy some wine and drink myself into oblivion and ultimately sleep. That turned out to be a good and a not so good decision later on.

It was quieter on my return – everyone seemed to be inside their vans cooking and eating. I breathed a sigh of relief and opened the red wine with a new sense of anticipation rather than desperation.

I was three glasses in, reading my book when the noise began again.

More music and screeching. Some wild dancing outside. Through my curtain I later saw a couple disappear back into their van followed hotly by another couple.

Four people remained outside, still gyrating and very obviously smoking weed. In a surreal move someone produced a ukulele. What on earth was this party, I wondered?

The answer came an hour later when one of the girls knocked my door.

"Sorry to trouble you. I'm Jacquie with a c and a q; would you like to join us?"

I pointed to my attire; a zebra onesie and a woollen beanie hat. "Er – thanks but no? I'm not exactly dressed for the occasion."

"A zebra?" she said curiously. "We're not into those, but how about being our unicorn?"

I didn't know what she meant, so ploughed on with my excuses.

"Besides," I added, "I don't mean to be rude but I don't know any of you."

That didn't seem to throw Jacquie in the slightest. She threw back her head and laughed. "Oh don't worry about that! Only four of us know each other," she said. "But that's the whole idea. This weekend is one big get to know you: if you know what I mean!" This was followed by a salacious wink.

I remember standing in the van's doorway as the meaning hit home. It was surreal, how I stepped away from my body, perfectly aware that one day this would make a hilarious story: how my camping weekend was crashed by swingers.

But as I came back to the moment it didn't seem that funny. I may have been a bit abrupt.

"No thank you. Really – cheers for the invite but it's not my scene at all. Have a nice time though," I added, rather lamely.

Jacquie made one last attempt to sway me. "Are you sure love? A tongue's a tongue when it's doing its thing …"

I slammed Myvanwy's door shut to make the point I wasn't

interested and distinctly heard Jacquie say, "Sorry guys. She's not up for it." This was followed by a groan of disappointment, a momentary pause before I was seemingly forgotten, and then the noise continued.

By then I'd started to feel quite uncomfortable. If I hadn't imbibed so much alcohol I'd probably have packed up and gone. But apart from it being illegal to drink and drive, I didn't trust myself to back the van off the levelling blocks, let alone ensure everything was secured away safely.

That thought prompted memories of a previous trip where, on a duel carriageway doing 60mph, an un-secured melon broke loose from the fridge and hurtled towards me like a cannonball. I could have done with something similarly weighty right now to throw at the swingers; maybe that would shut them up.

But really there was no chance. The rest of the evening continued on in a similarly noisy bluster with me unable to do anything but reflect on how much stamina they had for people in their fifties; their vans literally rocked for hours.

I continued the night alternately drinking or trying to sleep with a pillow over my head. Nothing helped. I then gave up and surfed the web. I even Googled 'swinger and unicorn', the response was as follows:

'Unicorns, also known as single women, are sought-after partners for many couples in swinging relationships; but, as the name implies, finding 'unicorns' can be incredibly difficult for most people.'

Exhausted and slightly hysterical with it all, Tim's words swam back into my head. 'Just think of the adventures you'll have.'

I laughed out loud then, realising I'd probably had enough for the time being. There would be more adventures in the future I was sure; but after this, it felt like it was probably the right choice to resume my career full-time.

CHAPTER 11: WHAT DID YOU DO?

I don't think Russ was overly-thrilled about my escapade with the swingers. He has a propensity to worry, and to him this just confirmed (from his perspective at least), how my life is riddled with near-misses and danger.

"I don't understand," he says with regularity, "how so many things just seem to happen to you?"

It makes me smile that we've had such different lives. He's been a company man and a family man. And obviously I haven't. He's had a regular wage cheque coming in, with which he's booked holidays during the school breaks. There's been routine partly because there has had to be, and partly because that's what he likes. In brief, he's risk-averse, and I'm an adventurer who, through so many jobs and experiences, has developed a different perspective.

It hasn't all been through choice mind you! On my life journey, jobs have been about survival. I had no real direction except for wanting to be an actress as a kid. When that was denied me, I just fell in and out of work (always working, but never focussed), sometimes several jobs overlapping.

Much as I hated the majority of what I ended up doing, I didn't realise at the time that I was gathering up new skills. Combined with the latent talents I already had, I was always able to keep my head above water and if nothing else, it's given me plenty of stories.

Not that everyone wants to hear them – I've come to the conclusion there's definitely a time and a place. One example when they weren't well received was on a visit to a very traditional family in Tamworth, an area with a large mining and industrial background as its heritage.

Through the process of chatting about their much-loved grandmother Rene, it transpired that every generation of the family, including the ones I was talking to, had led almost carbon-copy lives.

They'd all come from the same area and never left; they'd all been schooled in the same place; they'd all worked at the local factory and married young. They all congregated on a Saturday morning with the children for play and a chat; and Sunday lunch was always a family affair too. Holidays were of course always shared; at the same caravans at the same resort in the same week of every year.

Nothing wrong with that, although it didn't give much material for a eulogy. I was scribbling away, thinking of how to approach it, when one of them asked me about being a celebrant and if it was the only job I'd ever done?

Door wide open for me, I dived in and told them a few of my stories. Not too many, I'm always aware that the meeting isn't about me, but I did slip in a few sure-fire anecdotes that have worked previously, hoping it would lighten up the atmosphere a little.

So there I was, expecting some laughs and some words of admiration at my varied life and how much fun I seemed to have had. Looking up, I saw the opposite.

Every one of them, daughter, husband, sister and grandchild had edged slowly, imperceptibly along the sofa to get near to each other. There they were, clinging to each other like terrified laboratory monkeys, eyes huge, silently pleading with me to make it stop; make it stop now …

"Oh dear," said one of them, breaking the silence. "That doesn't sound like much fun."

I roared with laughter on the way home at how different we all are. There was me thinking I was being entertaining (more for something to say than anything else), and all they could see was the horror of my unstable, unwieldy existence. So just for entertainment, here's a partial list for you to enjoy or be appalled by. All my favourite jobs and lots more awful ones too. I hope they make you smile more than grimace.

1 Secretary; (both permanent and hundreds of temping jobs in medical, banking and insurance.) Skills acquired: How to type at forty mistakes a minute.

2 Pontins Bluecoat (a kind of holiday rep on a camp). Here I discovered how to use a microphone properly and to 'call' a barn dance; strangely enough, something I've never needed since leaving.

3 Tarot card reader. I had only one layout to offer and some very suspect interpreting skills, but did surprise myself on several occasions: once by spotting someone's affair; and another a pending court case. I told the man he was going to win, and he gave me a £20 tip!

4 Stand-Up Comic: This began in the 1980s when there were no female comics. It lasted eight years and included ten day tours around the mining communities of the North-East and monthly trips out to entertain the troops in Germany. It was *hard* and gave me a total breakdown at the end of it all.

5 TV Walk-On: Otherwise known as an extra, I've hung around in the background in studio-set bars; danced at discos; dressed up as a cow; been soaked to the skin by a water cannon for a building society advert and worn very unflattering period costumes.

The food on sets is great, the treatment is not and the wages are even worse; although I did once earn an extra £40 (as detailed on my wage slip) for 'cow capability'.

6 Actress: Small time. The only story here is of one lunch break when I joined the queue for food. An old man was behind me, so I made small talk as we waited, saying "Do you do much of this?"

He replied "Just a bit dear."

When I took the meal back to my table, a friend asked if I'd enjoyed my conversation with Sir John Gielgud!

7 Cruise Ship Hostess: Grandly known as Cruise Officers, our basic remit was to do the meet and greets and facilitate passengers to have a great holiday.

It took me two weeks to get my bearings on the ship; four months to conquer sea-sickness and six months to relax my mouth down from its permanent rictus grin, after my final contract.

8 Advertising: Freelance copywriter, blogger and creative. I still think my best proposal ever was for a range of chunky, chavvy watches from the 'Raid' collection. Sadly the client didn't go for it, but I had it all in my head: a poster featuring a male hand, slightly angled, fingers almost closed in a suggestive way whilst the watch remained fully visible. The strapline was to say: 'Raid. What your wrist was truly made for.'

I can't think why the client said no.

9 Songwriter: Lots of promises and 'this is going to be the next big thing' type of predictions, but in the end I had no major hits. However, I did have enormous fun writing with various partners in studios along the way. And a no. 48 hit in the top 100 in 1995. Get me!

10 Song Sifter: Now here's a job! Through the connections made via song writing, I once found myself listening to over three thousand entries for the Eurovision Song Contest.

I had to sift out the crap and put the others through to the next round, where the big guys, the heavyweight songwriters and producers would take over. Subject matter ranged from love; cars; dogs; polar bears; insanity and Krakatoa. I loved every minute.

11 Journalist: There's a surprise. Through a connection on a homes and interiors magazine I worked there as a secretary, then moved up to journalist doing small reports and shopping features. Ultimately I gained my own column (a whole page) in a Midlands-based newspaper called The Sunday Mercury.

The editor gave me a lovely strapline for under my picture: 'Ruth Graham. More Balls Than Your Average Bloke.'

12 Carer: For my dad with Alzheimer's and then for a friend's mum with the same. This lasted a year before the desire for writing returned.

13 Market Trader: With a grand announcement I left my job on a Friday, announcing that I was 'Going to sell posh lamps at Lichfield market.' The lamps turned out to be too expensive, and I didn't have the backbone to be standing in the cold all weekend. But my house is full of lovely lighting to this day.

14 Musician: I took up the violin in my forties; launched and managed an Irish party band for the next twelve years. Playing gave me arthritis in my neck but we had some wonderful nights. I'll never forget the topless lesbian dancing a jig at a Christening, of all places.

15 Publisher: The early 2000s saw me launch my own magazine; selling advertising in the day, and writing the content at night. All the skills I'd ever gathered in my life to that point finally came in handy. That formed the belief that nothing you do or learn in life is ever wasted.

And on it went. Loads more to list but before this turns into a badly-written CV I'll stop. It paints the picture that I'm a grafter and a trier. Something the Tamworth family more than got the gist of!

I also believe that the more we say yes, the more things we try and experience, the more we're exposed to life and other people. The Tamworth family were insular and happy that way. They didn't need exposure to other things, but I'm a personality that does. All the better if it's a little dangerous, challenging or risqué!

One of the most incredible of those stories was from the days on the ships, on what's known as a turnaround cruise. This is when the ship is changing itinerary and re-positioning for the season. In our case it was moving from the Caribbean to Alaska – a journey which took nineteen days and gave us plenty of time to get to know our passengers; something we didn't usually find on the normal week-long cruises.

There was a couple on board that turnaround who stood out from the normal selection of guests, mostly due to their mixed ages. He seemed to be in his late seventies, and she was no more than in her mid-thirties. Their interaction seemed strange as well. Too familiar and intimate to be father and daughter, but surely not a couple?

That question was answered one evening when the lady, Michelle, confessed in a drunken moment that she was a professional mistress, and the man, Carl, was her slave.

This secret was revealed in the main bar, whilst chatting to some of our team. Michelle, (who was very attractive with long blonde hair, huge eyes and naturally full lips), was alone, apparently having seen Carl off to bed. This allowed her to hit the Tequila big-style, as well as giving her a chance to chat freely.

"But," she added, "I'll be getting Carl up later, as he's not allowed to enjoy a good sleep. Today is punishment day, and he's been a bad boy."

I remember how we all just gawped at Michelle in absolute disbelief. The ship was a very free environment to say the least, but to our knowledge, we hadn't had a slave and a mistress on before. The closest we'd come to anything that random was probably when a conference of gynaecologists boarded, along with several hundred frozen vaginas to dissect; (chef had to clear the ice cream freezer and keep them in there until they were needed). But this was something totally new.

"I don't believe you," I said; speaking for our stunned group who mostly still had their mouths open.

"Come and watch," she invited. "Deck 11, room 207, at midnight."

I didn't go, I just couldn't face it. Too strange and cruel for me. But three of the entertainments team went; a few officers, the ship's comedian and even several passengers all hot-footed it to line up outside room 207 for the show.

I couldn't wait to hear the update the next morning from one of our team members. Apparently everyone had been let in very discreetly by Michelle, only to find this poor old chap on the sheepskin rug by the end of the bed, with some nipple clamps on, and some tiny chains around his balls, with little bells on (like you'd find on a cat's collar.)

My friend said what had struck her was the paleness of the old boy's skin, and how liver-spotted and frail he'd looked. It sounded awful, the poor man.

"But how did you feel?" I asked my friend. "Wasn't it embarrassing?"

She laughed. "Yes, at first. There was a strange silence in the room as it was all so surreal. But then he asked for permission to speak (apparently slaves always have to request this), and then he'd explained to the crowd, without making eye-contact, that it was his choice to do this. Then he showed us his thigh tattoos; the left said, 'property of Mistress Michelle'; and the right said 'slave to women'.

"And what then?" I asked incredulously. "I can't imagine how on earth it unfolded from there."

My friend filled me in. There had been a little light whipping apparently, and then Mistress Michelle had pulled off the nipple clamps, to which Carl had gasped and told her he loved her. I couldn't for the life of me understand what anyone got from this.

I got my chance to find out a few days' later at the pre-dinner cocktail party, when I found Carl alone. As he walked slowly over to chat, I saw several passengers looking around in a puzzled way, cocking their heads to one side as they tried to work out where the slight tinkling, almost imperceptible jangling sound was coming from.

He made it over to me, looking as always, at the floor. There was a silence, then I realised I was supposed to speak first.

"My friend told me she had an interesting time the other night. I hope you don't mind me bringing that up?"

Without a hint of a blush, Carl said, "Not at all. We come away on cruises twice a year. It's the only time I can have her to myself.

"Part of my role if you like, is to be humiliated, so we have the ideal captive audience on-board. It's quite the thrill for us both."

I wondered then who had been the mug. Who was taking advantage of whom? Before I could explore further, I noticed Carl was looking very pale and sweaty. I asked him if he was okay, and I'll never forget the response. Word for word he said:

"I'm fine thank you. But mistress has put nipple clamps on me. I hope she sees fit to remove them, or dinner may be quite an ordeal."

I asked him why he didn't just reach inside his shirt and take them off, to which he simply said, "You don't understand the rules."

By the end of the cruise I did. Carl lent me a manuscript he'd written about his life, and how he'd got to that point. It had all started as a young man when he'd married, and it turned out his wife had these tendencies.

On their honeymoon she'd chained him to the bed, left him with enough room to reach a toilet and a sink, but she left him naked, cold and without food. Promising to be back in a day or two she gave him an ultimatum. Either become her slave (!!!), or she'd divorce him and brand him as a homosexual (both illegal and a massive scandal back in the 1940s).

Plainly Carl had made the choice to obey, and so began his life of servitude. Incredibly, by day he was a successful company director, with a seemingly normal life. But in his spare time, God knows! This continued until his wife's death but even then, on the day of the funeral, her best friend turned up at the house and announced, "I've come to take over where Thelma left off!"

This woman turned into wife number two. A much crueller version of the first, who took delight in dishing out painful punishments and humiliation – even to the point where she organised a dinner party, invited several previous members of Carl's staff (including his secretary); and made him serve them dinner whilst naked.

The evening had ended on a tasteful note though, when they'd cleared the table and lightly whipped him. There really is no accounting for taste.

Sadly, when this wife died, poor Carl had been left all alone. He was literally institutionalised by now, having given up work to become a full-time slave.

He was incredibly lonely and there was no point to his life (as he saw it), so that's where he got in touch with Michelle's agency, and the pairing was born.

I got the opportunity to ask Michelle's side of it too, before they disembarked. What did she get out of it all?

The answer of course was money. Carl had paid for the cruise, and she charged a daily fee.

"It's easy work," she explained, "I don't have to have sex with him. I just spend time with the man. I order him around, do a few things to him to make him feel noticed and abused, and that's it. I wasn't cut out for office work, so this seemed the next best thing."

I laughed then, but she didn't seem to mind. I think Michelle could see the humour in that statement. How one could make the leap from 'office work isn't for me, but hey, I think I'll become a dominatrix' is yet to be explained.

But then again, it was a job that worked for her, and most certainly for Carl, so really, was anyone being hurt? I'm not sure the Tamworth family would have thought that way though.

Happily for me, Russ thought the story hilarious. Incredible, but hilarious. Telling him and watching his reaction, I was beginning to get a sense that behind his quiet exterior, was a man who was really good fun, with a bit of a naughty sense of humour, truth be told.

I remember saying to Russ that I hoped we'd still be having fun when we become as old as Carl was. How it made me happy to think I've found a partner, best friend and playmate.

“Me too,” he said with a wink, “Although if you don’t mind, we’ll give the bells and the chains a miss. You’re enough for any man without the added extras!”

CHAPTER 12: THE RETURN AND THE REALISATION

Oh the naivety (or possible arrogance?); imagining I could have an extended period of time off in Myvanwy and return on my own terms, to a full or even partially busy diary. The reality was nothing of the sort.

"Sorry, but we've got a lovely new celebrant," said one FD. Nice lady, thought we'd give her a try and it's working out really well."

"Who?" said another arranger, when I called to say I was back.

"Ruth Graham," I repeated. "I usually deal with Amanda. Is she there?"

"Ah," said the mystery lady, "I get you now. No sorry, she left a month ago. Do you want to speak to someone else?"

I told her I'd call back another time. I hadn't got the energy to start re-introducing myself after so many years on the circuit. The thought of trudging up yet more FDs paths with packets of biscuits and introductory leaflets in hand, filled me with horror.

More calls followed, during which it transpired that staff had changed at several more branches; and the revelation that one Catholic minister had actually spread a rumour I'd retired.

"I can't say who it was though," said the arranger.

I suspected strongly it was Father Damien from St Michaels – he's never liked the fact that celebrants say the Lord's Prayer if requested. I'm sure nothing would have pleased him more to see one fewer of us on the scene.

In fact, I want to ask him about this next time we meet. I want to ask if he's okay with retired clergy delivering non-religious content if requested, (because they do). And I want to ask how, if it's only those ordained that can recite the prayer (as he seems to suggest), then surely that excludes his congregation, most of whom won't be ordained?

One of my fabulous colleagues has a great answer. He says it's a minor niggle that many clergy carry with them "But if all else fails I tell them I'm a non-religious Anglomethobaptibrethresallycostal with Adventist leanings. That usually sorts it."

"Anyway," continued the arranger, "we're very glad it's not true and that you are still on the scene. I'll be in touch with you soon when something comes in."

I waited weeks for that call, during which time I had plenty of opportunity to reflect on the fragility of our work patterns. We're all familiar with the phenomenon of being flavour of the month one minute, then persona non grata the next.

I've been dropped like a stone for not giving one arranger a free service for a friend of a friend (outrageous!); and on another occasion an entire office of five ladies that used to give me work somehow decided I was earning too much.

On hearing about my purchase of the motorhome there was some terse comment about 'It's alright for some,' and the phone literally never rang again. Through their jealousy my invoices went from around £2k a month to zero!

There's also no rhyme or reason to the workflow in terms of death rates; and surprisingly, although busier than summer for obvious reasons, the winter season doesn't always guarantee a full diary. Even a colleague who moved to Canada has found this.

Based in Alberta, it was fascinating to read on our forum that over in the colder parts of Canada everyone generally waits until spring, as burials (which seem to be the preferred option) are so tricky in the sub-zero temperatures.

The same for the travel to attend them. Apparently many people will go four or five hours, covering over a thousand miles to get to a service.

As families are so far apart geographically they tend to combine the funeral with a family re-union, which makes perfect sense. It's interesting just how different our job is in other parts of the world.

But back to the UK; after being dropped so unceremoniously I guessed I had no choice. I was going to have to get re-acquainted with serious frugality once more. I wasn't going to burden Russ by asking for handouts, he'd got enough on his plate with the boys growing and needing new stuff all the time. I'd just have to suck it up.

This was nothing new, but slightly demoralising all the same. You don't expect in your late fifties to be relying yet again on reduced goods from the supermarket, eating dinner in a house you can barely afford to heat.

I did that during my twenties when I was working as a temporary secretary, unsure of when my next job was coming in. I did it in my thirties after I'd had a severe breakdown and could hardly leave the house, let alone earn any money. And yet again at the end of that decade whilst caring for my dad with Alzheimer's.

On a carer's allowance of just £65 a week, unable to claim any job seeker's allowance (because I wasn't free to look for a job), or any other type of benefit for that matter, I recall being about two months away from losing my home.

There's a vivid memory of walking into the sitting room seeing my dad eating a vase of lilies. He turned to me with pollen all over his face and just said "Fucking bitter. Horrible." It was that precise moment I recall entertaining the notion that the only way out was to kill him, myself, or both of us.

I was sick of the grind. Sick of living on cheap tinned meat and being cold to the bone whilst I ate it. I was tired of feeling ill, of having no support and nobody to hear me.

Fortunately that stage of the problem solved itself a month or so later, when dad went missing. Having tucked him up in bed and gone home for a hot chocolate and a good cry, somewhere between goodnight and the sun rising, he'd gone wandering.

It was a sickening, worrying, awful time but eventually he was located by the police shuffling along the hard shoulder of a motorway in the freezing cold.

The police traced me and informed me that he was in a mental institution, where he would stay until assessment. And that started off a whole new chain of events leading to (dreadful) care; mistreatment in several homes and his ultimate death. So when a family talks to me about guilt around someone's end of life story, I get it believe me.

Having lived in near-poverty so many times during my life it's given me a real appreciation of the good times and the value of the things I've worked hard to earn. It also makes me despair of how society has become with its throwaway culture and sense of entitlement – particularly with Millennials. Or is it snowflakes? I'm not sure but it's encapsulated in the story I heard recently about a friend of a friend, a lady who asked her ex-husband for an increase in child maintenance payments for their two teenage daughters. Yes they were all okay she said, but didn't he know how expensive their make-up and nails had become?

Quite rightly the dad refused. All the essentials were covered. His girls were warm, clothed and fed. He suggested they got a Saturday job to fund their beauty regime.

Appalled, the mother told the daughters the bad news. No increase in funds from dad. There was nothing for it; they were going to have to eat in at home three or four times a week now; to which one daughter dramatically replied, "So this is what we've been reduced to now is it?"

As a person who has endured very reduced circumstances at certain points in my life, I have no time for such nonsense. But I do despair for the future, for that hard-work ethic that seems to have been replaced by this sense of entitlement. I guess that's the prerogative of people when they get old and grumpy!

Eventually regular work did come back in for me when a couple of other celebrants left the area. And once again things went out of kilter. In the space of a few weeks a trickle turned to a flow and then an avalanche.

This is when Myvanwy came into her own. My accountant confirmed she could become an official asset to the business register and so in her new capacity as company vehicle, we began to cut quite a dash in the crematorium car park, where I used her for writing in-between services in lieu of sitting in a coffee shop.

Un-used to seeing such a large vehicle parked up it caused confusion at first. One mourner, mistaking me for a mobile café, knocked on the back door to enquire if I did bacon sandwiches? Another FD admitted he'd driven in and his first thought was 'Is it a mobile mortuary?'

Whatever the perception, it was a good conversation starter and a bit of a lifesaver for me as the workload got bigger and bigger. I also garnered a lot of repeat business from families served during Covid times.

It triggered a lot of memories for me, seeing them again. Particularly of the discrepancies I'd encountered during that period.

Like most people, I'd watched the news avidly and with trepidation. But even as the reported casualty numbers rose, I'd lost count of the times families privately confided that they weren't happy with Covid being stated as the cause of death on the certificate.

I always had to ask, more of an aside than anything, as it helped me shape the service in an appropriate way. I never major on the cause of death but obviously the words for a full and happy life would be different from a suicide or (God forbid) a murder.

At the time, nobody took offence at my asking, but many of them were angry when I raised the subject because of the apparent mis-classification.

"She'd had Coronary Obstructive Pulmonary Disorder (COPD) for years," said one family. "We always knew it was going to take her, so why they put Covid down as the cause of death we don't know."

Another family told me of how their brother had died in a car crash. Immediately afterwards, he was tested for Covid and that went down on his paperwork.

I remember being horrified. If I was seeing this then surely every funeral director; celebrant; humanist; vicar; priest; rabbi and Imam in the country would be too. This would amount to a massive tally week in and week out. Every single one of these mis-classifications was in turn driving up figures that dictated the country's policies and behaviour.

"Have you challenged it?" I asked one family, ever so gently.

They collectively sighed. I saw they hadn't got the strength, and it wasn't my role to push them.

This started a debate that even the mainstream were eventually forced to take up: questioning the difference between dying *from* Covid (as the genuine cause of death) to dying *with* Covid (as an incidental but not a fatal factor). But I'm not sure it ever really sunk into peoples' consciousness; everyone at the time was just too afraid and whipped up in the hysteria.

They probably didn't notice that at the height of Covid, flu seemed to disappear as a cause of death, in the general scramble to get figures as high as possible.

Alongside this blatant deception, we had to adapt as service numbers dwindled. I stopped delivering the service from the lectern; nobody could take any comfort from that gaping physical chasm between us. And I regularly made crem assistant Kenny work harder than he'd probably ever done; asking him to put out six chairs nearer to the coffin, in an effort to make things more intimate.

I remember how he tutted his way around the building, locating and placing the chairs in a semi-circle whilst half-heartedly 'sanitising' them with a rag that looked like he'd used it to clean up roadkill.

I also took to speaking directly to the families in the first person rather than the third, which I'd previously favoured. It even provided me with an opportunity to get them to chat and reminisce – a humbling if difficult experience, particularly the one I mentioned earlier with the photographs taped to the benches.

Another stand-out family was the case of where a much-loved mum died in hospital, unable to see her family because of the rules. (Rules later flouted by the UK Government at almost every level as they conducted their affairs and private parties.)

If that doesn't make your blood boil I don't know what it would take, but I won't deviate at this stage. The memory of this client is more because of the reason for the depths of his grief as he awaited the hearse carrying his mum.

I tried to comfort him at the crematorium door, but he was inconsolable. "She was ninety-seven and died peacefully though," I said. "I know things are difficult right now but what a wonderful life eh?"

Through his tears the poor man turned to me. I'll never forget his words.

"Yes," he said, "but they tried to cheapen it at the end."

I asked what he meant?

"They offered me money. The hospital Trust, to say it was a Covid death. Thousands of pounds."

I must have looked at him aghast, but had no time to pursue it as the hearse arrived at that moment.

All I remember is going through the motions, bowing to the coffin as it arrived; Kenny checking the coffin plate in his usual shambolic way, as the poor man next to me muttered, "My mother is *not* a statistic. She's just not."

CHAPTER 13: HANNELORE

Happily, one lady whose send-off created very different emotions, for very different reasons, was someone by the name of Hannelore Wright. I knew her just a little when I conducted her service; she was my friend's mum and we'd met maybe two or three times before she died.

My impression back then was of a slightly dotty old lady, with rheumy eyes and a life behind her. I regret that now: that I didn't ask her more, or indeed, show her more respect. She had such a story to tell, one we could all learn from, so with her daughter's permission I'd like to share it now.

A survivor of World War 2, Hannelore grew up in Gdańsk which was then a neutral corridor, one that both Germany and Russia wanted to conquer.

When the Russians broke through, things rapidly became brutal. Soldiers pillaged the villages, attacking the locals, raping and murdering the women and girls at will.

Hannelore's mother, feeling there was no way out and the only way to avoid such a fate was to escape, told her fourteen year old daughter she must leave urgently to try and reach her father's family in Germany.

Hannelore walked alone day and night, eventually reaching a port where she managed to stow away in the cargo hold of a ship (along with other refugees) bound for Germany.

I've no idea how she survived, or how long the journey took, but I can only imagine Hannelore was not in good shape on arrival. But again, there was no let-up. There then followed a three week walk to

North Germany, afraid to remove her shoes the entire time in case her feet became so swollen she'd not get them back on again.

During this epic walk Hannelore saw her first black American soldier which both fascinated and terrified her. She later also recounted tales of finding work in the fields en-route; of having only green potatoes to eat (food that even the pigs wouldn't touch). She recalled lying with a saucepan under her head at night so she wouldn't sleep too heavily and be late for work. The pittance she earned would then fund her travels to eventually reach her father's family in the North.

Whilst enduring all this, Hannelore didn't know that things were getting worse in Gdansk. That mothers were taking their children down to the sea, drowning their babies and themselves, in order to escape the soldiers.

She didn't know her own mother had gone there with her two brothers; only being saved by the youngest Siegfried, who begged his mother for 'one week more.'

Persuaded but terrified, Hannelore's mother returned home, but shortly afterwards took the decision to end it, first by poisoning her sons' food and then hanging herself from the kitchen light.

Unaware of the tragedy and unable to contact anyone, Hannelore continued on with her life, she simply had no choice. At the age of nineteen she saw an advert asking for nurses to come to the UK to look after TB patients, and that's how she found herself in rural Cheshire.

It's hard to imagine the racism she'd have endured, being seen as the enemy in such a small community. But Hannelore mastered the language and eventually went on to meet and marry a local farmer.

Somewhere in her early twenties she made contact again with her maternal family. Her brother Siegfried filled her in on the details, how he'd survived the poison attempt, and awoken to find his brother dead and his mother hanging from the light flex. It's no surprise that Siegfried struggled with outbursts of suppressed anger, in addition to alcohol problems for the rest of his life

And poor Hannelore. I can't imagine the mixed emotions: of

re-discovering what remained of her family, but also learning the terrible fate that had befallen two of them.

Hannelore went on to have two children, and then moved to the West Midlands, of which Birmingham occupies a large part.

I crossed paths with her daughter in my late forties; we formed a strong friendship and this led to a later meeting with her mum.

I always wondered why Hannelore was so close to her son and daughter; and why everyone did so much together. I'm ashamed to say it even irritated me at some stages, when I wanted to go out with my friend and she chose to be with her mum instead. Not having had that bond I couldn't understand it.

When Hannelore died I was more than happy to conduct her funeral, but still didn't know much of her story at that stage. I spoke about her love of family, her humour and the sheer hard work ethic – all admirable qualities of course. But it wasn't until the dust had settled, and the memories put into order that my friend opened up about the true extent of it all.

Then, I was honoured to be allowed to see the real Hannelore. It explained why she'd empty washing up water on the garden; take only short showers and a bath once a week and only put the washing machine on when there was a full load to do.

"Water is the most precious commodity we have," she'd say. She could also never understand why people would fire up their boiler for a few seconds just to heat water for a quick wash.

Hannelore was also a fan of boiling up a kettle and putting a flask nearby to store the excess hot water for use during the day. And as for the oven, it would never, ever be on for just one item. It had to be jam-packed or it stayed off.

I understood my friend more as a result too: how she'd inherited these eccentric traits that in fact were sheer common sense.

Most of all I finally understood what Hannelore had always said: how all that really matters is a roof over your head, and family to cherish.

That understanding made me really appreciate my new circumstances and how fortunate I was to have finally met someone who wanted to include me in theirs.

CHAPTER 14: FORMATIVE FRIENDSHIPS

Hannelore's story, as so many of the family stories I encounter, really underpinned the value of family love.

You'll have gathered by now that wasn't in my life, so friends have taken on a huge role in supporting me over the years. That said, it took a long time to recognise the difference between an entertaining friend and a good friend. At one stage I thought anyone who came out for an evening or made me laugh was in that category.

One of these was Jan. Brash and Northern with a heart of gold Jan was self-made. Her roots were barely buried, she'd never have cut it on the 'old money' circuit; but honestly? I don't think she cared. Her wardrobe was crammed with Armani and Gucci; she drove a nice car and ate the finest foods.

Jan was impressed by 'stuff', like the time we were out shopping when she saw an elegant woman wearing a beautiful scarf.

"Look at that," she drooled. "Vintage Hermes silk. I can spot it a mile off."

"But Jan," I implored, "don't judge a book by its cover. She might look posh but for all you know that vintage scarf might be covering up a bad case of impetigo! You just never know."

God knows why she hung around with me. I think Jan wondered herself from time to time, and occasionally she subtly let me know.

I distinctly recall being in the passenger seat alongside her one day. Apropos nothing she suddenly said, "Do you know. You're the only one of my friends who's poor!"

"You what?" I said incredulously.

"Well I'm not being funny," she said, "but I was just thinking as we were driving along. I could get a phone call and be skiing in Verbier tomorrow. But you couldn't do that, could you?"

Another of her classics was to casually hand me a gorgeous pair of over-the-knee black suede boots.

"Would you like these Ruth?"

"Wow," I said, "Thank you! Really? They're fabulous. Are you sure?"

"Oh yes," she replied, "It's fine. Of course I'm sure. It's just that my thighs are a bit too slim for them …"

Looking back, I ask myself why I put up with that kind of treatment. I toyed occasionally with dropping the friendship, but in the end things sorted themselves out.

Jan met a chap called Colin, and the two of them moved back to Yorkshire from whence she came. Well, I say moved, but it was actually more of a midnight flit. She left no forwarding address and nobody has heard from her since.

It came to light several months afterwards that she'd made off with the communal funds from the apartment complex where she lived. As treasurer, she'd been trusted to pay the utilities and ground rent but instead it seemed she'd been funding an extravagant lifestyle. I didn't feel so bad being 'poor' after that.

This issue, the one of being made not to feel quite good enough, raised its head again years later at a dinner party I went to. The short version of that very long night is that my then friend and I were separated (as were all the other couples) and placed at different tables.

I found myself seated next to Charles the merchant banker from Goldman Sachs; Philippe, who owned a vineyard in Portugal; Christine who was married to another merchant banker, and so on.

Without exception, everyone at the table but me was wealthy; well-educated; well-connected and English. Except on that occasion, through some sort of invisible signal that had passed between them all;

one that deemed me to be not quite worthy, they decided to conduct the entire evening in French!

They didn't even give me the opportunity to introduce myself. They just chatted and laughed in French; probably bullshitting about art and castles as they passed around the wine, overlooking me as if I wasn't even there.

So how to react? I had to bear in mind that I was at a large dinner party for eighty people. If I made a scene it would be embarrassing for everyone. If I attempted to strike up some conversation in English, it would just make me look needy, as if I actually wanted to talk to them. So I just sat there through two courses, until I could stand it no more.

I left the table and marched over to my friend.

"Tom. I'm being roundly ignored. It's bloody awful."

Tom looked at me dismissively. "Oh don't be silly darling. They're lovely people. What have you said?"

He turned away from me, distracted by the offer of some cocaine. I didn't even know he did cocaine until that moment.

I was enraged. "Give me the keys. I'll wait in the car until you're ready."

And so there I sat in the freezing cold until Tom had enjoyed dessert; more wine; cigars and doubtless more coke. Needless to say things didn't endure after that. I hated his friends and I hated Tom for not sticking up for me.

I've reflected a lot on friendship over the years for obvious reasons. A good one it seems to me, is one that can survive disagreements because its history is larger than the current problem.

I try to judge people on the vast majority of their behaviour, our history together, rather than the odd occasion when things are out of kilter. In fact, I think if a friend is behaving badly and it's not the norm, that's usually a sign they are in distress and need help of some kind.

Having said that, some friendships just never need tweaking. They're easy and they flow from week to week, sometimes with minimal contact, sometimes with daily calls, but either way you always know it's there.

My friend Darren fits into that category beautifully. I credit him for keeping me here with daily calls and check-ins when life was too much to bear. He's a beautiful soul with a sensitive nature and a genuine desire to help and is adored by everyone who knows him.

Those qualities describe Tim perfectly too. Definitely a man prepared to turn up and lend a hand like he did with my motorhome, but always ready for a chat; steadfast, loyal and hugely funny. That's why it was so devastating to lose him in March 2022 at the age of just fifty eight.

It was a short battle with advanced cancer that came out of nowhere, combined with some very poor treatment in hospital. Had the nurses actually looked up from their mobile phones and noticed he'd had a stroke whilst in his bed, maybe things would have turned out differently.

Incidentally, I heard a similar story from another family whose dad had a heart attack whilst resident on a hospital ward. They told me of how, despite his pleading, nobody would take him seriously, so he ended up calling emergency 999 for help from his bed!

For that family, and of course for Tim's partner Tracey, there are strong questions to be answered by the relevant hospital trusts. But Tracey didn't feel strong enough to do that at the time.

Instead, we all just focussed on giving Tim the best send-off possible, so once again I called in the amazing ladies Fran and Carrie from A Natural Undertaking, the funeral directors who really do things differently.

In the time Fran and Carrie have been established, the market is slowly changing. Maybe they're the ones changing it. Either way people are realising that they don't have to have the standard thirty-minute service at a crem if that's not what they want.

There are plenty of other options regarding venues and what happens within the service – and that's exactly what was done for Tim.

The first thing Tracey looked at was transport. As Tim was a gardener, she thought it would be amazing if he could reach his final destination in the open trailer that he'd towed around nearly every day of his working life.

This required some logistical thinking for Fran, who made several visits to measure up the trailer and then return with a pair of specially made clamps that would keep the coffin in place. Tim would be driven around on a tour of his home town of Sutton Coldfield, past all his drinking haunts and the park he loved so much, so it was vital everything stayed put.

Finding a venue was a little harder. Trying to convey the idea to people that we'd be doing an actual funeral in there (as opposed to just a wake), seemed to blow some people's minds.

"What? You're going to have a coffin in the room as well?"

"Yes. We don't need the tea and biscuits. It's the actual service."

"In the village hall?"

"Yup. Like I said ..."

Eventually Tracey found an understanding vicar who let us use his church hall. Hired for an entire morning this gave us the freedom to do a non-religious un-rushed service in a way I think Tim would have heartily approved of.

And so, on the 1st April (a date that wouldn't have been lost on Tim), he turned up at the due time in the trailer, decorated with rows of beautiful flowers, and a Union Jack. As a proud Englishman with an interest in local history, he'd have approved of that too.

Hundreds turned out for the celebration of his life. School friends, drinking friends and people from the vintage and 1940s re-enactment scene that they were so into. Gardening clients came along too, and one of his best friends from his youth even flew over from New Zealand. That's how loved he was.

God knows how I got through the service. Just looking at Tracey, vacant with grief, almost floored me. And I've no idea how his step-daughter got through it either. She gave the most brilliant tribute to

Tim: full of fun, laughter and happy memories. And like all good eulogies, everybody got to learn something too.

I never knew the story about how he was out on a gardening job one day and had forgotten his cutlery for lunch, which happened to be noodles. Unfazed, Tim just went to the local chemists and bought a pair of toothbrushes instead! But he was like that, able to see a way round everything. He invented and built things. He lived for cool cars; motorbikes; stylish fashion; his friends and his relationships with Tracey and her daughter.

I held it all together for the service, focussing on Russ who was sitting at the back. He'd only met Tim once so was there more to show his support for me, but by the time we got to the graveside part of the service, he'd had to go back to work.

And that's when I cracked. I didn't want to let Tracey down but just couldn't stop the tears from flowing. Tim was the first person I've really cared about that I've lost.

We may have been trained to 'not steal' a family's sadness at such a time but on this occasion the sadness was justifiably mine too. It was everybody's that day. We all still miss him. But everybody who knew Tim will never forget. And for those of you who didn't have the privilege of knowing this amazing man, I'd like to invite you to get to know him now though this little poem that I wrote for his service:

OUR TIM

God he could talk!
How the words they would flow.
Face to face or the telephone, on he would go.
"But I'm rambling he'd say", before more inhalation,
then unleashing a torrent of yet more information!
Local history: The Streather-built homes Lichfield Road,
The farmhouse torn down, now a family abode,
The Village Stores, "Now an accountant's," he'd say,

And you remember the family that all moved away?
You know, the one where the woman had a son that divorced,
then two of their children ended up in the courts?
And the lady at Sainsbury's that married the son?
By this time you're cross eyed, not a clue where we've gone!
But joking aside, our wonderful Tim.
What didn't he know?
Where hadn't he been?
What couldn't he do, what hadn't he made?
An extraordinary man, at home with a spade;
a mower, a spanner;
His dog, his motorhome, beer glass, or banner.
So many aspects in his 58 years,
though he lived in the past for many of these.
Wasn't he dapper in his zoot suit and hats;
Or military outfits; polished-up spats?
With Trace by his side, looking stylish and glam.
A wonderful couple; our gal and her man.
Not ones to gush, but oh boy what a pair,
Invincible, solid and always both there,
Should you need some advice, or friendship or muscle,
You'd just have to call, he'd pitch up, "Sure, no trouble"
Part of our fabric, part of our lives.
Tim is ingrained in our stories and times,
That we've all shared together, along with our Trace.
We'll never forget him, he won't be erased.
Too much to remember, too much to recall –
His stories all funny, factual or tall.
His drunken impressions, his searing sharp wit.
His direct summations, 'I'm not doing that – it's shit!"
A man of integrity, a heart made of gold.
When Tim Maddocks was made,
They sure broke the mould.

CHAPTER 15: UNFORGETTABLE

When I wrote the first book, I chose the title 'A Thousand Goodbyes' to reflect the number of services I'd more or less done. It's probably around half of that again now: something I find hard to believe at times.

Russ says he doesn't know how I do it. If he's referring to the energy needed, then to be honest, I don't either. Some days involve delivering multiple services, family visits and writing too.

Throw into that the normal demands of running a house; walking the dog; staying on top of paying the bills, taxing the car and making sure I remember to slap on my HRT patch (Mondays and Thursdays) then it's a bloody miracle to be honest.

Alternately, if he means how I manage the emotional demands, then it's because there's a professional distance, helped by the fact I didn't know the deceased. I mean look at how I crumbled at the end of Tim's service. If that was me in professional mode every day I'd never work!

Nobody would want a celebrant sobbing over the coffin; they want someone to get them through it. So I manage it through a mixture of mindset; acupuncture (for physical stress); the occasional counselling session and neuro-linguistic programming (NLP), a form of psychotherapy that focuses on the relationship between the mind, language and the resultant behaviours.

It's used to help break negative or destructive patterns; to create an awareness around a problem, behaviour or situation. Simply broken down, it apparently takes twenty one repetitions to create a habit.

We all have our routines and repetitive behaviours that dictate our outcomes.

For example – think about someone overweight wanting to lose a few pounds. Imagine a lady coming in from work; slipping off her shoes, throwing down her bag and automatically reaching for a bottle of wine. She then pours it, wanders through to the living room and plonks herself down on the sofa. Here, she takes several glugs whilst texting or calling up friends.

Within an hour she's absent-mindedly finished the bottle. By this time she's slightly sozzled and possibly ravenously hungry, so off she goes in her weakened state to raid the fridge.

And so the cycle continues: tired at the end of the day; eating and drinking too much; being ever more tired because she's not eating well or focusing on health.

NLP would aim to introduce a set of behaviours to change the patterns and make her more aware, as much of her behaviour is unconsciously locked into the routine.

So now, maybe the routine would be broken up to make her think differently. She may come through the door and be encouraged to insert something new into her pattern. Perhaps after throwing off her shoes she'd repeat a mantra, something like 'I am strong without alcohol'; or 'Do I really need this tonight?' Maybe she'd have made a pact not to text friends whilst eating or drinking; it's only an activity to be done without food or drink to supplement it. Perhaps she'll not throw off her shoes but keep them on as a reminder that she still needs to stay in 'focus' mode for a bit.

It's a lot deeper than that in reality, but finding some way of breaking patterns and anchoring positive behaviours really does work. To help with control of emotions when I get to the crem, my safety mechanisms are to have read through the service multiple times to the point of boredom, and to consciously not talk about how sad or tragic the person's demise has been with any of the staff (even if it's heartbreaking).

I also have several back-up mantras including: 'This is not my grief' (because in truth, it's not); and 'You won't work again', which is another strong one. The third is a reminder to myself that I am an ugly crier. Truly I am. Who wants to look at a snot-ridden celebrant with eyes puffed up like vol-au-vents?

Even revealing my professional methods, Russ still thinks I'm amazing. Conversely, I tell him I think he is. How he supported his wife through a fourteen year-long cancer journey, and then nursed her single-handedly through her final months, all whilst working from home and caring for his boys.

How he was then able to stand up at her service and deliver the eulogy I don't know. If it was me mourning a spouse I'd want to be sat there with no responsibility except for bawling my eyes out.

"It's because it was the last thing I could do for her," he says.

I can see the strength behind his quiet exterior. Russ is not an Alpha male, determined to force through his opinions or demonstrate his manliness, but he does have steely resolution on certain subjects. This was obviously one of them.

Then I asked how he was doing. Does he miss her?

He says yes, but her voice is fading in his memory now. He mainly grieves for what his twin boys have missed out on, losing their mum when she was just fifty-five. Before she passed they both had to tell the boys the honest truth; that she wouldn't be there for prom nights or their graduation or wedding days.

I watch Russ's face and I honestly can't imagine how it must feel. Then he tells me that mixed in with all this is the guilt he feels for loving me, and the fun we have together.

But wasn't that what he wanted I ask? Wasn't that what drove him to get out there in the first place, because he didn't want to be lonely?

I tell him just because he's moved on doesn't mean he has to forget; that would be impossible. We can sit side by side, she and I. I'm okay with it; there's no jealousy here.

That conversation then sparked an idea for a little sideline – it's funny where inspiration comes from. This idea came to fruition remarkably quickly, thanks to knowing the right person at the right time.

Cat is an adult storyteller/performer who I know from my old days back in cabaret. She's found at Blenheim Palace near Oxford most Halloweens, holed up in the spooky cellar, weaving stories about ghosts and witches. She writes books for children based around magic and she teaches and performs storytelling and writing all over the world.

Equally as important, she's a dab-hand at pitching for grants from the UK Arts Council. After liaising on the idea, rather brilliantly, Cat put together a proposal for a show based around death awareness and the celebration of those we loved. Just a month or so later 'Unforgettable' was born.

The offering was in two parts: through a mixture of stories, comedy and music we proposed to show people how to celebrate those they've loved and lost.

Using material from my work, we'd teach people to ask the important questions like, what have they given us? What have we learnt from having someone in our life? Through the process we hoped it would help people celebrate life and talk more openly about death as part of a natural cycle.

The second part of the offering was that we would run writing workshops, with Cat teaching people how to write a story, and me teaching people how to gather information to write their own eulogy. In brief, they'd be challenged to look at their lives and what they'd done with them. It would also get them talking to their own families about arrangements and funeral wishes; (often referred to as 'The Big Conversation'.)

The Arts Council liked the pitch and the fact we were going out into the community to try and engage people around such a taboo subject. Months of feverish writing then ensued.

Initially, it seemed like there was so much to talk about: my work as a celebrant, and the things I've seen and done. But then I realised a lot of it was very personal, and to display it for public entertainment might be betraying some confidences. So then, it was a question of a broader approach – taking my own personal stories and weaving them into some kind of a message.

To say the next few months were tortuous would be an understatement. Crafting the show was like giving birth to a headstone – sideways. At times it seemed impossible, and definitely painful, but at the twelfth hour we got there.

Ultimately the show was a huge success. As we toured libraries and the occasional theatre, people listened to the sad stories and laughed alongside us with the funny ones.

I challenged them to write their bucket lists in the break, and then come back and share their ambitions with each other. They sang along with Cat to some of most popular funeral songs (My Way, Time To Say Goodbye, Thank You For Being A Friend, Stand By Your Man), and on the workshops they shared ideas, achievements and challenges they'd overcome.

I was humbled by the variety of people who attended the workshops; from the lady with nine children who'd run a regimented household and turned every one of them into fine, upstanding citizens; through to the lady who had been born blind and been the first-ever person to receive an eye operation that gave her sight. From the Oxfordshire therapists who'd attended en-masse to learn more so they could help their clients deal with death, to the lady so crippled with a fear of death, she'd never allowed herself to live.

To a person, the feedback was amazing. Described as 'uplifting; thought-provoking; poignant and life-affirming' we closed our final show on a high. Afterwards, on my drive home I considered how, although we may not have won any awards, the reaction to what we did was enough in itself. And once again it was clear to me that all of us in the industry are, in our own little way, effecting change and hopefully improving others' lives.

And that includes people in lesser-known roles, like that of the death doula (also known as an end of life doula). This is a community-led role that's very much a vocation, providing loving, practical, emotional and spiritual support (if required) to the dying person and often their families too.

It's not something many people have heard of, as death has become so sanitised in the western world, but historically people acted in this role for many hundreds of years in their homes and communities. It's just we've forgotten how to talk about death; how to help people have meaningful and peaceful transitions and that's what doulas are now bringing back.

I know of several friends who would have benefitted greatly by having someone to guide them through all the decisions and choices that need to be made at such a time, particularly as end of life is such a lonely journey.

Professor Allen Kellehear talks about this on the End Of Life Doula UK website: of how just 5% of the journey for a dying or grieving person is in front of a professional. In other words, 95% of the journey is taken alone. Doulas exist to fill that 95%: people from all walks of life who want to be part of compassionate communities to change thinking and behaviours.

It very much depends on the person or the family when and how a doula comes into their lives. If it's in a voluntary capacity, this may be through a hospital; hospice; care home or community group. In a private paid capacity it could also be in a person's home, where a doula can be useful throughout three distinct phases.

The first phase is planning for the actively dying moment. Is it important for this to be at home with family, able to touch and see your loved ones? Or on the flipside, maybe the person's priority is to fight with everything they have, to hold on for as long as possible, trying any measures or alternatives to sustain life.

Phase two is actively dying and this would be discussed and clarified with the doula about what that means. The topics may cover things such as having visitors, being able to control that space (as one of the last things you can do). The dying person may not want people sobbing over their bed. They may want people to enter the room with positivity and gratitude, or they may not want visitors at all. Many people prefer to be remembered when they were in better health, and that's perfectly understandable.

After death comes phase three, the reflections with loved ones on what it all meant. Often these selfless people haven't had time to really see what's happening, they've been so immersed in caring. They're encouraged to then be present for themselves and their own emotions. To notice their surroundings again; to undergo any meaningful rituals they may need, from visualizations through to reading poetry.

I can't think of anything more beautiful than having someone to guide a person and their family through these stages, particularly as the hospital system and any semblance of real care appears to be collapsing in the UK. This is highlighted almost weekly on the family visits I make, with dreadful stories of people who, quite frankly, would probably still be here had they been looked after better.

But back to more positive influencers, and another little-known offering in our world; that of a charity called Brief Lives Remembered. Run by a wonderful lady called Paula, this is another branch of 'our' industry that people wouldn't generally stumble across unless they were in particular need, but one that plays a vital role in helping people to heal.

Paula helps parents of stillborn babies who never received formal burials. Their mothers often have harrowing stories like my own mum; of their dead babies being removed immediately after delivery, having never had a chance even to hold them.

Worse still, back in the fifties and sixties, some mothers were returned to maternity wards shocked and bereaved but yet still asked to be a wet nurse for other peoples' babies if their own mothers couldn't produce any milk! The lack of empathy and understanding is almost inconceivable.

As I saw within my own family, parents in these circumstances are left in limbo. They never move on, not knowing where the baby's final resting place is. This causes immeasurable anguish to the mothers, who carry their grief for decades, often until their own deaths.

Brief Lives Remembered deals with enquiries from parents or twin siblings within the UK. Working with minimal information, (sex, name, parents' names, gestational age, hospital they were delivered), they use parish records to discover what happened to the child.

These babies are often traced to un-marked graves or sometimes they were buried along with an adult female. But regardless, it's the finding that matters; the closure of the agony of not knowing. Finally they can end the search.

I had the honour of doing such a service when a lady called Daphne located her baby through parish records, (amazingly, something she did on her own). It transpired that the child was buried with other children, which had been semi-expected, but still took her mum some time to come to terms with.

However, after recovering from the shock Daphne tidied up the area, turning it into something resembling a grave. She then placed a memorial stone there, and asked if I would mind conducting some sort of service.

I said it would be my pleasure.

The challenge was to create something meaningful, bearing in mind the enormous time lapse, but I did my best. Discovering a beautiful song on YouTube called 'The Hardest Goodbye' by Lucy May Walker helped me too (the video is incredibly moving, do watch it). We played it by the graveside and afterwards I spoke the following words:

"Baby Zoe. We didn't get to meet you, but the knowledge of your time on earth has left its imprints on those who loved you, and you were never forgotten.

"You touched your mother's life indelibly. She carried you every day of your existence; and she mourned you every day after your loss. You have never been forgotten.

"Whilst that gap could not be filled, finding you will now close the circle for your mother. But first, we need to honour and recognise you as the child she nurtured inside of her.

"I formally name you Zoe Claire Reynolds. We give thanks for your soul and your spirit. For the comfort and hope you gave to your mother as she carried you.

"Your presence here will serve to remind us always of the power of love, and the importance of family. May you rest in eternal peace, Amen."

I then presented Daphne with a certificate. Just something I'd made at home, but she burst into tears when I gave it to her. She'd said previously how difficult it was that her child's birth hadn't been registered; as if all those months she was carried, and the trauma of her loss counted for nothing.

Daphne hugged me and said she'd treasure it for the rest of her life. To some, that would have been just a piece of paper. But to her it was validation of her child and her loss, which had finally now been acknowledged. It was back to the importance of things being witnessed again.

Together with the resting place found, Daphne could now permit herself to live the rest of her life in a less troubled way. She and the baby were now, in some way, re-united and she had finally found peace too.

CHAPTER 16: A NEW PERSPECTIVE

Peace is the feeling that most people seek above all after a loss. And one of the strongest examples of its power came about eight years into my career, when I thought I'd done it all.

This story is of a lady called Marguerite, who'd achieved a magnificent one hundred years. But the trouble is, when you have no children, and your partner is dead, there's frequently nobody to mourn you.

Fortunately, Marguerite had one good remaining friend called Debbie who was considerably younger, so Debbie and her daughter Hilary intended to come along.

They provided me with some basic information, and I did my best to pull a service together, but it did worry me that having approved the service in advance, they were already aware of everything that would be said. It felt strange that I'd be parroting back to them what they already knew so well.

When I met the ladies on the day, Debbie seemed very tense and anxious. We chatted beforehand and I thanked them for making the long journey, to which Debbie replied, "There was no question of it. No matter how far away, we'd have come. She was too beautiful to leave this world alone." But even as she said it, I got the sense of tension and definite sadness. There was something underneath that I wasn't yet aware of.

That tension niggled me all the way through, as I did the introduction (that they'd already read) and followed on with the first poem they'd chosen. Then it came to the memories section. Something in the back of my mind told me I had to do it differently. There were just the three of us in chapel – it didn't seem right to be doing it the traditional way, I didn't feel the ladies would get anything from it. So, ignoring my pounding heart, I went completely off script and gave Debbie the chance to speak.

To start it all off I simply said: "Debbie. You told me here that you met Marguerite thirty five years ago when she came to visit the neighbour. But you haven't told me how. What facilitated that meeting?"

She looked up startled, and then quickly smiled as the memory was stimulated.

"It was through the dogs," she said. "Mine ran over to hers across the drive and we just got chatting."

"Oh, so she was an animal person then?"

"Yes," responded Debbie, "Very much. And we used to go to the donkey sanctuary in the park on a Sunday, and then out for lunch."

And that was it; Debbie was off. I heard fresh memories that were being stimulated purely because they were being given the freedom to air. Debbie and her daughter even chatted to each other during the process, often laughing about something just remembered. They told me some of the gossip they'd shared, and of Marguerite's love for the finer things in life.

In the process of it all Debbie also shared her guilt: the source of that anguish I'd seen earlier upon her face. Of how she'd moved away and tried to find care for Marguerite before going; and of her subsequent sadness that the home Marguerite ended up in didn't turn out to be so good.

"But you tried," I said. "You did your best, within the timeframe you had. I know exactly what it's like as I had to do the same for my father. We don't know what happens behind the glossy exterior of the brochure, but you must forgive yourself Debbie. You got her settled as much as you could before you moved away."

"Do you really think so?" she said, with tears in her eyes.

"I know so," I responded. "You did so much more than many others would have done. Please take that on board. And now I'm going to leave you and Hilary alone with Marguerite for the last song, and I'll see you shortly outside. Say everything you need to. Take your time ladies."

I watched Debbie through the window as she spent her last moments with her friend. She walked over to the coffin, placed a hand on it and said her final goodbye. Then she came out to meet me, looking like a different person. Her eyes were bright and she was smiling as she held my hand and said thank you.

"Do you feel better now?" I asked.

"You have no idea," she smiled. "And now we're off for some champagne."

CHAPTER 17: WHO DO YOU THINK YOU ARE?

I hope that may be one of the things people remember me for one day; as a facilitator of good feelings. As I mentioned a couple of chapters ago about eulogy writing, it's important that we leave good memories.

So, having brought this up again, it would be churlish not to include the information for your own use. This could be adapted to writing a eulogy for someone else, but the main focus is on producing one for yourself. (This is something the afore-mentioned Oxford therapists were proposing to adapt to work on with their clients).

If you're not keen on tackling this now, then skip to the next chapter, but if you do fancy it, you'll find it's a powerful exercise. Not only for looking back and recognising your achievements, but also for looking forward and seeing how your remaining time may best be lived.

Part one is all about gathering the information and content.

Exercise 1: Getting To Know Yourself

Write a list of adjectives you'd use to describe yourself.

Now write a list of adjectives you think others would use to describe you.

Are there any differences?

(Do others see you in a better or worse light)?

Why do you suppose that is?

Do any of these things need addressing in your eulogy?

(Setting the record straight perhaps. Or explaining why something happened so that other people have a better understanding of you and decisions you may have made.)

Exercise 2: Achievements: (Looking beyond the obvious)

We have certain things we as humans use to measure our 'success' in life. Generally these are based on our relationships with others; whether we've married and had children; what kind of career we've had etc.

But success is actually very subjective and can include many other types of achievements. For example it may cover:

Overcoming a negative habit or addiction.

Positively impacting on others; through kindness, example, selflessness; bravery etc.

Persevering on despite very difficult odds. Or managing to view a situation positively where others may see it in a different light.

It could also be a physical success like learning a new sport or skill, or achieving great results in the sport. Don't be modest – if you have climbed a mountain then let people know.

Whatever the achievement or success, this is your time to be celebrated.

Exercise 3: Gathering Quotes

What have people said to you along the way? Is there anything you could use to back up some of the information you'll use later?

Have people ever told you you're kind/inspirational/brave/clever/helpful etc? Or have they praised you for something you did?

Make a list of the comments that may be useful.

Also use quotes from famous authors/poetry etc that you can incorporate to demonstrate a point, or to measure up against.

For example the writer Maya Angelou said, "People will forget what you said; they will forget what you did, but they will never forget the way you made them feel."

How have you made people feel along the way?

Exercise 4: On That Date In History

It may help to give a sense of perspective on your story by linking it to historical information if appropriate. This helps to explain why things happened or the choices people made:

For example, UK children in the second-world war generally tended to have an interrupted education, which accounted for why so many ended up working in factories and doing manual jobs.

Emotionally they frequently fell into two categories; either those who struggled to show outward emotions to their children and families, preferring to demonstrate their love through doing and providing rather than saying. Or, they were the other way – super doting; adored their families and lived for them. Because of what they'd been through they knew that people mattered far more than material things.

What was happening on the day you were born?

What were the fashions / music etc?

What was the political climate? And the cultural one?

Did any of these things direct or change your outcomes?

Exercise 5: Anecdotes

This is the space to talk about unusual happenings; funny stories and/or outrageous events.

It could be about the day you met your heartthrob. Or spent your life savings on a caravan. Maybe you've saved a life, or made a room full of people laugh.

Anecdotes and stories are to underline a point, and to bring warmth to a life story.

Exercise 6: Hobbies / Interests / Travel etc.

Include these to demonstrate a work/life balance. And again, any achievements associated with them.

Exercise 7: Friends / Relatives

This section is a chance to thank people who have been special to you for their impact on your life. Or to relay any particular stories associated with them.

Exercise 8: Learning From Your Example / Your Legacy

I sometimes ask people what they've taken from having someone in their lives. One young teenager said about his grandad that he'd seen the way he'd handled conflict – and from that, he himself had learnt to be a 'man'.

What will people learn from you? For better or worse.

Alternatively; what advice would you give them to help them live better or more fulfilling lives, based on your own experiences?

FINAL QUESTION:

If you died tomorrow and someone asked your nearest and dearest if you were happy with your lot, what would they say?

How do you plan to change this if it's not a 'yes' answer?

PART TWO – THE WRITING

Where To Start? The traditional chronological method is about telling your story in the order it happened. But don't forget to warm things up with a few anecdotes.

Rather than 'Charlie was born on the 16th July 1932, the second child for parents Roy and Joyce, and a younger brother for Ron,' try and paint a picture as an opener.

'There's a crowd of children cheering on a fight in the centre of the playground at St Martin's school in Coventry. As usual, Charlie Scraggs is in the middle – defending the honour of his younger brother.

'This kind of loyalty was typical of Charlie, who put family above all else his entire life. It was also typical of the generation. Those born between the 1920s and the 1940s tended to have morals, manners and a strong backbone. They stood up for what was right, and if that meant being involved in a few scuffles for Charlie, then so be it.

'His mum Joyce remembered' .... (and on it goes).

Another approach is to talk about someone's themes and traits. For example:

'Hilda had a laugh that filled a room. Some of you may remember the time at her 60th when her best friend hired a male stripper. We all heard the laugh that night didn't we?! But that was Hilda – always fun and always great company to be around.'

Or: 'Loyal, funny, kind and generous. Just a few of the qualities in Laura that you will all recognise. But she was also a fabulous cook. So many of you here today will have been lucky enough to receive one of her celebration cakes as a gift. I've a particular memory of the time that' …

There are many other approaches but this is probably enough for now.

I hope you've found it useful. I still refer back to this exercise on the days I feel I'm falling into a writing rut. Everyone deserves a sparkling story for their last goodbye, and that includes you!

CHAPTER 18: FINDING JOY

The natural progression from writing about how we'd like to be remembered was of course to think about how I'd be remembered. I'm not everyone's cup of tea: I'm not subtle, some would see my directness as being rude, others love the fact I call people out when there's something I perceive to be wrong, unfair or just not right.

This was demonstrated fantastically on a trans-Atlantic flight when I was placed next to a large chap who manspread across the seat, encroaching into my space. I've got nerve problems in my neck and shoulders, if they're compacted it triggers migraines, so I knew this position wasn't sustainable for twelve hours, or even twelve minutes.

He then called the air hostess over several times, loudly fussing about newspapers, luggage and special dietary requirements. Several of the passengers were already looking and tutting, logging him down as a potential troublemaker.

Inexplicably, he then put the overhead light on fully into my face and relaxed back into his chair, hands behind his head, completely unaware of the huge patches of sweat on his shirt. I knew we weren't going to get on.

As I was contemplating how to tackle all of this, he suddenly turned to me and said, "You may like to consider moving your book over a few inches."

I saw a few heads turn; I could tell ears were tuning for my response. I didn't disappoint.

My response was simple: "And you may like to consider using some deodorant."

Let's say it was an uncomfortable journey for everyone, and from there I decided never to fly long-distance again. But yes, this propensity to not put up with things can be divisive. It has lost me friends, but I hope that whoever I've known, whatever state our relationship is in when I die, they'll at least give me credit for humour; the ability to laugh and also provide some fun along the way.

Finding joy in life is incredibly important, especially in this line of work. It can threaten to consume or even destroy, so any opportunity to have fun or to try something new, with the added bonus of a few laughs along the way, is always a big yes for me.

The work in stand-up comedy back in the 1980s was one source (although when you do it for a living it's more contrived than natural), and some nights are not fun, believe me! But real, natural, spontaneous laughter and the joy of making connections with like-minded people is what truly feeds our souls.

That's why lockdowns were so hugely damaging to people. The sense of dis-connect was massive. People were literally withering and deteriorating without access to their routines, company and conversation. Proof if ever it was needed that we need this elusive joy.

I've sought it out in many ways to get me through. The tamer attempts have included yoga (which brought calm, when I remembered to do it), and a fair amount of suppressed humour at the gas content of the class. There's nothing like a room full of older ladies, triumphantly expelling wind whilst in the 'downward dog' position, as everyone pretends nothing has happened.

This trait is so British; being embarrassed about something but covering it up by non-acknowledgement. From saying a big emotional goodbye at the end of a reunion, only to find out you're then walking in the same direction to the train station so you've got to start chatting again; through to waving madly at someone you think you know but don't (and then you have to stare into the distance and keep on waving at an imaginary speck on the horizon); we've got it down to an art.

But yes, some of these yoga classes were a treat. It was like being on the football terraces at an international match – a room full of vuvuzelas sounding off. It got so bad at one point the class teacher had to put on some whale sounds to cover it up.

Another attempt to find joy was through hard exercise – a bootcamp that saw me getting up at 5.15 am; exercising by 6 am for an hour, and then crawling home to start my day. That lasted three months: (frankly I'm surprised I did that long), but sadly, it wasn't the 'thing', that elusive drug to keep me going.

I then tried something completely different and started applying for TV quiz shows. Much to my great excitement, I was accepted on The Chase (the UK version with Bradley Walsh who is fabulous). This gave a fantastic insight into how television works behind the scenes.

But before I talk about that, first I confess I've been on TV before, in 1987 on New Faces, a variety talent show which back then was the equivalent to Pop Idol or Britain's Got Talent. It literally drew around seventeen million viewers each week, so it was a really big thing for me.

The event was divided into three days and two nights, staying at the now defunct Birmingham Holiday Inn. Day one was a light rehearsal for the purposes of camera and lighting and then shopping for outfits in the afternoon.

Day two was costumes and rehearsal and day three was dress rehearsal with the full house band and then the live show in the evening.

I remember even back then being a bit suspicious of how it was all put together. The acapella group of singers were complaining that they weren't allowed to perform the song they wanted to; someone else wasn't able to wear the clothes they'd chosen; and I wasn't allowed to do vocal impressions 'because someone else did that last week.'

I wondered surely they had singers every week? What was the problem with two female impressionists? The producer told me to go away and stop making a nuisance of myself, which left me feeling very deflated and sure I stood no chance of winning.

That was confirmed later in the evening at the dinner in the hotel's private suite. The table had been laid out with name cards in advance, and I decided to swap my name around to sit next to my new friend, a talented Welsh pianist called Fiona.

We were jabbering away quite happily until halfway through the meal when the producer, by now red-faced and obviously tipsy, clapped his hands in a very affected way whilst loudly shouting, "Which one of you bastards has changed their place card?"

Silence fell over the table. He let it linger, perfectly aware of everyone's discomfort, before asking again, every word enunciated slowly as if we were hard of understanding.

I couldn't bear the tension any longer. Very meekly (like Oliver Twist asking for more), I said, "Me. It was me. Is there a problem?"

Well – that set him off. Yes, there was a problem, apparently. The table had been laid out very carefully so that a crew member sat next to an act, sat next to crew and so forth.

"I don't know why you felt yourself so important that you had to be moved," he continued. "Anyway; don't think you've got any chance of winning now dear."

With that, he turned back to his conversation, leaving me choking with shock on my bread.

"Oh dear," said Fiona, "I don't think he likes you."

That was proven over the next couple of days as I was bullied, and bossed around, and my script changed almost hourly until my head span.

The final draft arrived one hour before filming. Two thousand people were due to fill the Birmingham Hippodrome to watch me fail, and I'd never felt so sick and nervous.

To my credit, I did get through it looking confident and professional. I delivered the comedy with timing and aplomb; the only problem was, the panel hated me!

They hated the dress I'd been told to wear and my material (the material I'd been forced to do); a pile of hackneyed and occasional racist one liners. It dawned on me then how manufactured television is – performers really do have very little say in how they appear.

The creative industries really are nothing like they seem from the outside. When you look at a polished show, or hear a song of great beauty, the chances are there is unpleasantness in its history.

Stories abound of people being trampled on or bullied, or in time-honoured fashion ripped off (like Van Morrison for example. He never received a penny from one of his biggest hits, Brown Eyed Girl.)

For my own part, one of my most disappointing and infuriating experiences was during the songwriting years when a publisher, full of enthusiasm for my talent and ear for a good melody (their words) signed me up for a couple of years to sell my music.

I was promised all sorts of things – they'd pitch it to everyone from Whitney Houston to Barbara Streisand, maybe even a film title song! Mentally I was already spending the royalty cheques as the ink on the contracts dried.

So what happened? The answer of course was nothing. I'd fallen prey to a common practice, when promising artistes and writers are head-hunted and signed to agencies in order to keep them out of the market.

This is done so that their own artistes (the ones on the official books) aren't threatened by newcomers: they can continue to thrive if new talent is kept out of the way. Like I said, showbiz/television/radio is a cut-throat experience all round.

That said, my experience of being a contestant on The Chase was hugely pleasant in comparison, although there's still an element of deception. There's no audience for a start: the clapping and the laughter is all canned. The studio is also tiny, not anywhere near as spacious as it appears.

Three episodes a day were filmed so it was all very tightly run (no wonder on some episodes Bradley Walsh looks absolutely knackered), and whilst we were waiting for our turn, we were very tightly managed.

One element of our day was to be taken into a room and 'coached' in how to look happy and appealing, "Not like this" said the chief researcher, flicking on a showreel of people who looked like they'd just been sentenced to death.

"Try for a smile rather than a grimace," she continued, "and just chat to Bradley like he's a normal person. He'll make you feel welcome."

We had a few practice goes on some buzzers, and answered a heaps of questions and then were taken to our individual dressing rooms to wait.

This was the interesting bit, an obvious tack to ensure we got no opportunity to consult together on a game plan. No chance to decide between us that if something hadn't been answered in a second, one of us would take responsibility to pass and move on to the next thing.

We also couldn't leave the room without an escort in case we bumped into a Chaser and slipped them a few hundred quid or tickets for a new life in Panama, you know, just to tip the balance in our favour. So yes, it was all tightly controlled, but understandably so.

When we finally got on set (the last filming of the day), everyone was hyped up and totally ready to go, but it became apparent I was playing with three risk-averse contestants. As player number three, I decided to take the gamble and risk it all, taking on the Chaser for the big money – £45k!

I'm proud to say at this stage that I won it. I beat Paul Sinha (The Sinnerman) and took it back to the team. He also proved to be very sporting, and when a question came up that was similar to one he'd encountered before, he stopped the filming and called for another, just to make it fair. Proudly, I beat him thanks to a mix of general knowledge that just worked out on the day, and a teeny bit of luck.

Ultimately our team played for a £55k jackpot, the combined total of our efforts. But thanks to the numbskull next to me, we lost the lot. I won't forget the question that sealed our fate: 'Where on the body do you wear a bobby pin? His answer was, 'On a nappy'. I have just about let go of my irritation at his stupidity.

Sadly, on shows like this you don't get a compensation prize, or even a bag of jellybeans to take home. It really is all or nothing, so having stared my share of the jackpot (almost £18k) in the face and thought of how much it would have changed my life at the time, it took a couple of days to get over that.

What the experience did do for me though was provide a bit of a lift, which kept me going for a while and gave me another story with which to entertain my friends and colleagues.

But the thrill faded as it always does and the melancholy kept re-appearing. So on I ploughed; hanging off the high wire at Go Ape to find my high; taking up belly dancing and eating too much (not at the same time.)

As a Libran it's a common mis-conception that we're balanced individuals, whereas in reality, for most of us, life is a constant search for this state. It didn't take a genius to see I was out of kilter once again.

Eventually, peace came. Not in the form of a life change, but a mind change, prompted by an article about gratitude. Quoting the Zen teacher Zoketsu Norman Fischer it said:

We take our life, we take life, we take existence, for granted. We take it as a given, and then we complain that it isn't working out as we wanted it to.

When we see ourselves and everyone else as separate atomized individuals with needs to be filled, we can become overwhelmed by all the unfilled needs. So we think we should just look out for Number One, me. But if instead, we see the world as a place of belonging and connection, we are not weighed down. A mind of gratitude will help with this.

It was a simple but timely reminder that I had forgotten to be grateful; for my skills and my circumstances. I have a beautiful home, good friends and someone who cares for me at last; who loves me with every fibre of his being.

Just as importantly, I've got work that is meaningful – I really do make a difference. A card I once received came to mind at that point.

The card where a family thanked me for how I'd dealt with their mum: it ended with the words, 'We Will Never Forget You'.

Remembering that card and the other lovely words I've received sent a rush of warmth through me. I was doing okay. And maybe I'd answered my own question as to how I'll be remembered.

If it includes the words 'straight-talking but fair; good fun; hard-working and honest' then I'll take that. With thanks and of course, a touch of gratitude.

CHAPTER 19: IT'S ALL IN THE SLOG

Doing the 'Unforgettable' show and appearing on The Chase were both good experiences for me. It put me back out in the public eye and turned into great preparation for a little publicity campaign to re-market my first book. The one that had taken an eternity to write and about five years off my life along with it!

I still remember the painful writing process and how, if I'm really honest, I'd indulged in many classic distraction techniques along the way, just knowing the volume of sheer graft that lay ahead. A book is a very different prospect from a service, which can be written and polished in a couple of hours with experience; but this was a very different beast.

It took a bit longer still to get going, but after I'd hacked off my hair and spent two months moping about it; and after I'd had another go at decoupaging a table and learning the harp, there was nothing left to do. I forced myself to get cracking.

This turned into a year or so of drafts and re-writes; edits and corrections; getting confused about which draft I was working on, then discovering after three weeks it was the old, abandoned version. I remember the frustration and the sinking feeling, and how I frequently felt it wasn't worth the effort.

At that stage I was just jaded, wondering how on earth prolific writers managed to spew out a novel a year? I still do actually, but I guess the answer is probably that when someone gets to that stage of success, they have more time to devote to their art, and perhaps a raft of people to help them along.

But that wasn't my path back then. Flying solo I opted to gather together my recollections, jot down notes and develop a keen eye for the touching or the absurd (all good material I thought); whilst still endeavouring to keep my eye on the ball and give every family I was dealing with one hundred percent of my attention and professionalism.

Once edited and proofed it was then time to find a designer. This entailed a whole new learning curve. Font size; finished book size; front cover design and page layout; for several weeks this language became my daily diet.

I'd never really thought about it before but we all know that feeling; the one where you pick up a book, turn to the back cover, read a little and think 'Yes, I'll just have a quick flick through.'

This is the vital bit! How a book 'looks' inside is the decider as to whether you'll take it home and read it or not. It has to sit comfortably on the page and the spacing has to look right.

I didn't know it at the time but there are two approaches: technical and artistic, and you do need someone working alongside for this. If you plan to write a book yourself then don't scrimp at this stage as I believe it really shows in the end product.

Everything pulled together in due course, but there was no time to rest. There was then publicity to take care of. Secretly, I was pretty pleased with myself that I'd come up with the bright idea of tying in the launch with 'Death Awareness Week'; a wonderful seven days of talks and interactive events aimed at opening up the conversation around death; all hosted by the charity Dying Matters.

This subject is something I've banged on about for years, having had so many experiences of families unprepared for the event. So yes – what better way to link together a subject I'm passionate about, and the launch of the project that had taken so long to come to fruition?

That connection to the charity week and the book also provided the 'hook' for my press releases. Initially entitled, 'Celebrant Taps Into National Conversation Around Death And Mourning', these releases were carefully crafted and then launched in the direction of anyone who would listen.

I sent them to Radio 4; BBC1 and BBC2; ITV; The Guardian; The Express; The Daily Mail – you name it. Each one slightly tailored to appeal to the target audience, I was confident there'd be some pick-up but there was nothing. Not one shred of interest.

The countdown to Death Awareness Week ticked on; I began to despair. All that time and money invested and without publicity, nobody was going to see it. Was this destined to join all the other projects I'd attempted over the years? Manuscripts; plays; music and songs – just sitting in a drawer gathering dust.

My lovely friend Darren decided to step in and help. He pinged over a Whats App, along with a picture of an article going viral in the papers. It contained the picture of a skinhead, looking folorn, holding up some packets of candy. The headline read:

'Pouring Popping Candy Under My Foreskin Was The Biggest Mistake Of My Life.'

"This is what you need bab," said Darren. "Something a bit more sensationalist. People have short attention spans; think creatively."

I racked my brains for something funny, with instant appeal. Something I could talk about without revealing too much client confidentiality.

After many hours, I landed on it. I'd use one of the stories from my first book, the one about a group of Rasta mourners deciding to have a 'recreational' smoke – quite forgetting they hadn't released the ceremonial doves by the graveside.

So yes; I now had my headline, which read: 'Stoned Doves At Rasta Funeral Ruined My Career'. Surely that would do it?

But sadly, there was still no take up.

This is the difficulty of being un-connected. I remember a chat with a wealthy, well-educated friend a while back, who told me of how, after leaving Cambridge, doors 'just opened' for him because in that world, somebody always knows somebody who moves in the right circles.

Had he wanted to do anything from trade commodities, through to climb the ranks in the army, or enjoy a stellar career in TV, it would have been his for the taking. But me? I was so badly connected in the early days when I wanted to be an actress that I didn't even know what city held the building that housed the room with the casting couch inside. Now that's un-connected.

In the end, after ninety-seven press releases, countless emails and many phone calls, I got myself an interview on local radio with a man who doubled as a Dolly Parton tribute act, and a burlesque artiste. She (chosen pronoun) went by the brilliant name of 'La Femme Fresh.'

It turned out to be a really great conversation with La Femme, moving naturally from serious to amusing and back again. We spoke about the need to talk about death, and to plan for the inevitable. And the stoned doves story of course, and of changes in attitude to funerals, and how they're often now more 'people-centred' than formal and/ or religious.

"So give me an example of a really unusual funeral then Ruth," she said. "What kind of things can people do that are different from normal?"

That was a gift of a question, so first I told her and the listeners about some of the more sensitive, beautiful things we can do. I mentioned the outdoor funerals in peaceful settings and then went on to the story of a village hall service where everyone had a butterfly Post-It pad given to them.

During the reflection music, they wrote their messages then got up and placed them on the coffin. By the end of the service, it was a glorious, shimmering focal point, all those butterflies glinting in the sunlight. It really was the most spectacular sight.

"You see," I explained, "It's all about choice. Funerals aren't legal services – they're not bound by rules, so if a family wants to think a little differently, they're perfectly able to put together something personal that reflects their loved one in the way they'd like. Occasionally though, it does go a bit askew."

"In what way?" asked La Femme.

I then told her about a debate raging on our celebrant forum, one that centred around bad language, and how a family had requested that the celebrant use the 'c' word during the service, as a nod to the deceased's fondness for it!

This had sparked lively conversation on the page but in this instance, every celebrant had come down totally in favour of absolutely not using the word.

For my part, I'd shuddered at the very thought. I could just imagine some of my FDs faces if I'd tried! But incredibly, when the day of the service arrived it hadn't stopped the family from having the word spelt out in flowers.

I thought La Femme was going to pee glitter laughing at that story. Even more so when I finished it off with a flourish, describing how the family, struggling to find a reputable florist prepared to do it had ended up 'having a go' themselves. The FD later described them as being 'A bit crappily done to be honest.'

I tell people that story and it takes a while for them to believe me. But like I said earlier, because there are no rules around content of services, there's freedom to 'celebrate' a life in a totally individual way, no matter how inappropriate or offensive it may seem to others (like the Nazi funeral story I told earlier.)

The switchboard lit up as I told that story. The producer through the glass screen looked delighted. 'Best figures ever,' he told La Femme through the headphones.

The producer then made a circular sign with his hand in the air, to continue talking, so I took the conversation onto a different topic, making sure to keep it lively and controversial.

Moving on to naming ceremonies (another strand of the family-led services that we offer), I told them about an event for a little boy called Otis and how, over a Zoom call, his parents Dyson and Aleah unveiled their plans for his 'special' day.

Firstly, as a nod to dad's East London heritage they wanted to dress Otis as a Cockney Barrow Boy. And then, as the climax to the ceremony, they wanted to pierce one of his ears.

I remember asking if they were planning to have him branded too?

"You wot?" Aleah had snarled. "Why is everybody so down on us? It ain't illegal!"

"But it's incredibly painful for the child," I said. "How can this be a 'special' day for him?"

"He's ours and we'll do what we want," she'd screeched, simultaneously leaning forward into the camera, all over-tanned cleavage and pancake face.

She'd then given me the bird, frozen in time for a second before the screen faded to a blank.

Aleah left me a review on Google shortly after saying in 'Heinz sight' (sic) they wished they'd never been in touch, and that I was 'judgmentalist' and unkind.

Stunned though I was, eventually it became just another bit of material for the next book, or in this case, a radio show. La Femme hooted at that story, and the switchboards were off again. The interview ended with another plug for my book, and I went home on a high.

I checked my sales figures on Amazon the next day. Twenty five copies had sold overnight; I was absolutely elated. But it really does go to show the power of the media, and what a bit of exposure could do. Had I got into a national newspaper, or on a TV chat show, it could have potentially changed my life. And having such an irregular income from funeral work would have ceased to be a problem.

But for then, I was thrilled to have sold twenty five more copies. I wasn't the next J K Rowling, but for someone so unconnected, for a moment, it really did feel like the next best thing!

In due course though sales did pick up. I simply hadn't yet discovered the world of the virtual book tour; a magical place where professional promoters offer out new releases to other bloggers to review online. They hate it and you're doomed; but if they love it? Well, things could change forever.

I was directed to a lady who usually specialised in romantic fiction. Happily though she was intrigued enough to say yes. She asked me for a promotional banner and some blurb, a sort of synopsis that would tempt in potential readers.

She then sent out the clarion call to her database and amazingly twenty eight bloggers said yes thank you, they would like to review 'A Thousand Goodbyes'. So out went the copies followed by the agonising wait for the reviews to come back in.

And when they did?

'UNPUTDOWNABLE AND THEN SOME!'

'HILARIOUS MOVING AND TOUCHING'

'MUST READ'

'WONDERFULLY HONEST AND SURPRISINGLY UPLIFTING'

It had all been worth it. Books began to move; more reviews came in and I was on my way.

Honestly? I could have wept with joy.

CHAPTER 20: THE THINGS LIFE THROWS AT US

I suppose the lesson of perseverance is the main take-away from that last story. Had I given up at any stage the book would never have been finished, published, reviewed or selling.

I'm not sure whether we're born with the skills of perseverance or whether it's something that develops out of sheer necessity, but possessing it has seen me through some pretty rough rejections. I wonder how today's kids would cope with the following examples:

"Your accents are unconvincing, your dialects appalling and there is no future for you at the BBC."

(The response to my audition for voiceover work.)

"You. The purple lycra zeppelin. Get off my stage!"

(Shouted by the choreographer during my un-trained attempts to be a 'dancer' at an audition for Andrew Lloyd-Webber's musical 'Cats'.)

"We cannot offer work to older ladies at this current time."

(A letter received after looking for promotions work in the local department store: I was twenty three!)

"If you gave your manager a blow-job you might get a bit further. Your figures this month are crap!"

(This delightful piece of advice was offered to me by my superior (allegedly) as we were out in the car trying to sell advertising space in a local newspaper.)

"Don't worry about the cellulite. Good lighting will sort that."

(Stripped down to my underwear, I was auditioning for a shower commercial in front of a table full of men. Never, ever again.)

"You've obviously worked hard on the book. But we don't like it as much as the original, so it's a no. Sorry."

(This was after a four month re-write at the publisher's request. Aaargh!!)

"Too short and a bit on the plump side."

(Seen written on my application for Britannia Airways back in the 90s.)

And on it went. But this is life, isn't it? Surely one has to develop resilience and teach our kids to be the same way, rather than wrap them up in cotton wool until their mid-twenties. To my mind that's a sure-fire way to produce kids with no social skills and no confidence.

The lesson of perseverance and tenacity is one of the things I hope to pass on to Russ's kids when they feel close enough to let me in (and when they forgive me for encouraging the chores chart!)

I see them struggling with schoolwork and friendships; getting downhearted about the slightest of knocks, and although I know it's normal mid-teens I'd love them to really get the concept of 'the more you put in, the more you get out'. But like I say, we're not there yet; my words and advice fall on deaf ears. They still treat me with polite tolerance, and I still struggle with anticipating and dealing with the needs of a teenager.

I also don't understand how anyone can need four meals a day, plus huge amounts of snacks. I don't get why someone would develop the urge at 9pm to start playing the drums with which to entertain the rest of the household. I don't see the need to wear ear buds all day and night. And as for their reasoning: why would anyone go back to bed after taking a shower in order to 'let my deodorant dry.'?

These things irritate and bemuse me in turn but then I take heart from the philosopher Aristotle's words who said:

'Teenagers these days are out of control. They eat like pigs; they are disrespectful of adults, they interrupt and contradict their parents, and they terrorise their teachers.'

Reading that, I think actually they're not too bad at all. Perhaps teenagers are a conundrum to all adults (parents or otherwise) for a certain amount of years.

Then I switch the focus and try to put myself in their shoes. How it must feel to be a family with a link missing in their chain? Then one day, a random soul who is nothing like the person they lost, gets plucked from somewhere in the universe and steps in to fill the gap. Absolutely rubbish is my guess.

We still don't live together (another eight months has elapsed since first declaring that). We've shared a summer holiday and countless weekends but I still think it's kinder on the boys that I'm not invading their space, and it's gentler on me, someone used to living alone for decades.

We will blend together in good time. I just hope they're pleased for their dad that he's met someone who makes him happy, as deep loneliness is a dreadful thing.

Living alone for so long taught me to live with that state which over the years has varied from mildly niggling to crippling. During one of the lockdowns it was so bad that I even downloaded an ambient track from YouTube entitled 'One Hour Of Coffee Shop Background Noise.'

Checking back on the video's comments I see I'm not the only one who used that strategy. But even during such desperate measures, I had to laugh. Amongst the general background buzz, mixed in with a few discernible phrases, ('Happy birthday mate!'; 'Oh that's too hot!'; 'No it's my turn to pay'; 'That's awesome') was one very loud lady from New York. She got on my nerves to such a degree that I had to leave before I'd finished my imaginary coffee.

But knowing the depths loneliness can take a person to always makes me more empathic, particularly when I visit someone who has just lost their long-term partner and has no family to fill the gap. I'm always happy to spend the extra time chatting, long after the official interview process is done.

One man that springs to mind is called Leonard. "My wife, my life," he used to say. He showed me pictures of them over the years, the two of them ageing gracefully and simultaneously but the spark between them still leapt off the page, whatever the decade.

"I literally have no plans for the rest of my life," he said sadly. "She was everything to me. We couldn't have children, so I'm on my own now." Then he paused, looked at me with tear filled eyes and asked the hardest question ever.

"Could you tell me what the point is? I'm not sure any more."

Sadly, I couldn't. The poor man's best years were behind him and we both knew it. I wondered if it would be a story of one of those couples who die shortly after each other, as they simply can't go on alone.

But whatever the sad outcome, Leonard had obviously been one of the lucky ones who chose well. Unlike the lady called Sammy who contacted me about a vow renewal. We met in a local pub and I heard all about her and Terry's relationship.

"It's a shame he's had to work today Ruth" she said "because we could have just decided on it here and now. But anyway, it gives me chance to give you some of the honest background."

The first layer she unveiled was how they'd had problems in the early days 'blending' their family; she had a girl and a boy, and he had three girls. There'd been everything from cat fights, to inappropriate behaviour with her son and one of the step sisters.

I thought then how nothing is ever perfect. Thank goodness I haven't got kids to throw into the equation with Russ and his children. At least we don't have to shoehorn a family together.

"Anyway, we got over that bit," Sammy said. "My boy's now in prison, so that got him out of the way," she continued casually, "and the girls have mostly moved on. It's caused a lot less tension in the house, and Terry hasn't hit me for over a year, so I thought that was worth celebrating."

I nearly choked on my drink. I wondered if she'd want that little gem including in the renewal script?

"I know what you must be thinking," she said, "I'm a fool and all that. But people don't know what he's like when we're alone together. He's a totally different man."

Those words made me shudder as thoughts of Vinnie sprung to mind: the classic dual behaviours of someone who controls a relationship.

I didn't take the enquiry in the end, it would have felt wrong under the circumstances. I couldn't preside over their ceremony knowing a history like that, so I just told Sammy I didn't think I was the right celebrant for them and wished them all the best.

That's another aspect to the job. Because what we do is so personal, you really do have to gel with the family, and it's our prerogative as well as theirs to say no if something doesn't feel right.

I had the same feeling about a service for a beautiful older lady called Aileen who'd met a handsome young African waiter in Tanzania. (Are alarms ringing yet anyone?)

Having brought him home to Birmingham, she installed him in her house and about a year later I went to meet them. In the farcical display that unfolded, she explained how they'd met and 'fallen in love'.

All the while her husband Gil (short for Godlisten) nodded amiably along. He smiled a lot, and laughed in all the wrong places as she was telling their story, and it was plain he didn't have a clue what she was going on about.

What on earth, I wondered, could their connection be?

"Humour," she said immediately. "We laugh all the time, don't we Gil? We laugh in bed, out of bed, at the supermarket – everywhere in fact. And look at him; who could resist. He's an Adonis!"

This must have been a recognisable phrase for Gil. He instantly beamed and flexed his arm muscles accompanied by a heavily-accented invitation to "Look At My Strong!"

I did the wedding for them at a reduced price because it was plain they hadn't got a lot. I did my best to inject all the stardust and fun as usual, but the jollity in the room was forced. Gil had nobody there on his side, and all of Aileen's friends could see what he was really about.

Rather predictably, once Gil had his permanent residency in the UK, he filed for divorce. Aileen had to sell her little house, no longer full of laughter, to pay him off.

She did her best to recover but she was financially broken, heartbroken and not a little embarrassed at how it all turned out. She committed suicide a few months later.

Again, just like her wedding, the service felt more like we were going through the motions. I spoke about celebrating Aileen's life and giving thanks for everything she'd left behind, but there's no way the atmosphere could have been anything but sombre. It always is in these circumstances.

CHAPTER 21: TOO YOUNG TO DIE

If Aileen's service was bad enough, it was nothing compared to the absolutely dreadful day that I was called upon to do three services in a row, all for young people under thirty who had taken their own lives.

'Died by suicide' is now more the accepted term but even though every one of them had this factor in common, the circumstances couldn't have been more different.

At the 9.30 am service we gathered to remember a young lady who'd had mental health problems for many years. When she was well she was the life and soul of the party. She was fun, glamorous and incredibly creative.

"But then on a bad day," said her mum Layla at our meeting, "she could clear a room. The darkness of her mood could be toxic: you could literally feel it like a physical thing."

I understood what she meant. We've all walked into a room with an atmosphere and wondered what on earth has gone on beforehand. (In my case my natural refrain is to wonder what I've done, but that's just my insecurities again.)

"She also became incredibly destructive," added Layla. "She smashed up the house once because I wouldn't give her the car keys when she was drunk. We had to get the police involved and it was an absolute nightmare.

"She's balanced on window ledges threatening to throw herself off and even held a knife to her grandma's throat. If I'm honest we were all as terrified of her as we were for her."

I could sense Layla's exhaustion and bewilderment. And the struggle she was having to make sense of her daughter's loss and what her life had been all about.

Layla suspected her daughter Annie had undiagnosed ADHD and was possibly bi-polar, but the family had received no help. They simply supported Annie as her behaviour lost her job after job, partner after partner and home after home.

"In the end we stopped looking forward," said Layla. "We had to take one day at a time as the long-term outlook was too bleak."

I understood that sentiment at least. It took me back to caring for dad with his Alzheimer's, when I'd been considering my own lack of options. I remembered the exhaustion and the feeling of hopelessness. And the relief when he had finally gone, mixed with guilt at the relief.

But no matter what the circumstances, Annie's service still had to be a celebration of her best bits. And as a massive fan of hats, everyone was instructed to wear one as a tribute to her.

It was a fabulous sight on the day, where trilbys sat alongside fedoras, wide brims, fascinators and sports caps. You name it, it came out in remembrance of Annie's life. There were tears and laughter at her antics, and some beautiful music. But when it was all over, I ached for her mum inside.

Poor Layla hadn't had the closeness with her daughter that so many bereaved parents have. She hadn't got solid memories of their bonds that would see her through into the future and sustain her. I waved Layla off with the heaviest of hearts, and headed back to the chapel for the second service.

I won't dwell much on this one, as Benny had been a loner without any family. He also didn't have much of a back-story. All one of his few friends was able to tell me was that Benny liked gaming; eating pizza; and his cat.

Benny's decision to leave this earth had come about because his first and only-ever girlfriend had ended their relationship and, as explained in his note, he couldn't imagine life without her.

I did my best with very little information (and of course I never talk about the circumstances or the motives – that's too personal). But despite trying my best, the service lasted just ten minutes and was attended by three people, none of whom was the girlfriend.

In direct contrast the third service was for a beautiful young woman, we'll call her Cleo, who was a super-high achiever. She played instruments; spoke languages and had the world at her feet. To everyone she seemed popular, talented and secure in who she was and where she was going.

Sadly, all it took was a couple of blips with her exam results for Cleo to feel she'd let everyone down.

The utter tragedy of this was the girl's university had known things were wrong. It transpired she'd made a cry for help attempt the previous year; but nobody had informed her parents! Not one person displayed the courage or common sense to think this young woman may be in need of some parental help, advice or love.

The excuse? She was eighteen and deemed to be an adult. Plus a sprinkling of 'client confidentiality' and general data protection. All the usual bullshit that authorities use as an excuse to hide behind.

Cleo's mother was determined to make her death stand for something. She talked about campaigning when she felt stronger, to get things changed. "Anybody in education away from home should be looked out for," she said. "If parents can't be geographically close, we have no choice but to trust our kids to authorities. And we've been let down."

However, before Cleo's mum could even begin to recover, we had to face the service. She wanted that too, to stand for something: to have some kind of message that hit home. So, after the introduction I continued:

"Cleo's parents have chosen not to cover up what happened. By being honest about this it's hoped that it will encourage anyone else going through any issues – school related or otherwise – to reach out and seek help.

Cleo hadn't got the life experience under her belt to know that things always turn around. That even when things seem overwhelming or hopeless, there is an answer or solution. But you have to give life time to reveal them.

So, if one thing is to come of her loss, it's hoped that it will be the encouragement to reach out and talk. To buy time to see a better alternative."

And I guess that takes me right back, in a very rambling way, to the start of the previous chapter and the observation about perseverance; something I've learnt through doing this work and my own experiences, is essential to our survival and success in life.

At the end of that morning I remember feeling desperately drained. I staggered out of the chapel exhausted and ready for bed, even though it was still only lunchtime, but the day had one more surprise element in store for me before I got home.

Reaching the car park I bumped into one of my favourite FDs Charlotte. We had a chat about a recent funeral we'd done for a child under sixteen.

As with baby services, these are also provided free to the families. The celebrant donates their services gratis; and the funeral company, whilst doing it free for the families, then claims back a large percentage of it (up to a certain fee), from the local council. The long and the short of it is, the family doesn't have to pay for anything unless they're ordering extra cars, flowers or something very extravagant like a horse and carriage.

"Was this the family who launched a Go Fund Me page?" I asked.

Charlotte confirmed it was. Set up in the child's name to help pay for funeral costs, it had raised around £6k.

"But hang on," I said. "If the funeral costs are picked up by the council, then ....?"

Charlotte raised an eyebrow. "Precisely," she said. "We went round to deliver the boy's ashes yesterday. The house was a right shit hole apart from the one room. Brand new carpets, freshly decorated, a new suite. They'd literally just finished it all the day before."

I was aghast. On the way home I pondered on what sort of people would profit from their child's death, and the generosity of those kind enough to try and help them?

Happily though, on the subject of teenagers, we are finally making progress on the domestic front. The boys have moved on from polite indifference to something warmer and more accepting. They ask me how I am when I pop round; and they actually let me make suggestions as to how things might be done or improved.

I've shown them how to make an omelette; and a decent home-made soup and a roast dinner (quite a step up considering they didn't know how to boil a potato before I came along.)

We've been shopping for prom suits; I taught Kyle to sew on his school badges and dropped him off at a last-minute party. His brother and I have spent some time playing guitars together, me showing him the chords to Led Zeppelin's 'Stairway To Heaven' and him playing along.

It may be my imagination, but I think he looked at me with a new sense of respect when we did that. I wanted to say 'See – I'm not the old duffer you think I am!' but that would maybe have sent us one step backwards. Instead, I just grinned at him, told him well done, and to keep it going. I genuinely think he's got the makings of a really good guitarist.

Through all of this I've observed Russ watching on from the sidelines looking happy and hopeful. They're not kids to show huge amounts of emotion, so I just take it where I can. I'm never going to be a step-mum; but I can definitely be their friend, if they'll let me. There's definitely a thaw, and I'll take that for now.

CHAPTER 22: RESOLUTION

In the end, it took a sixteen-year-old boy to move things along, in the most uncomplicated of ways.

It happened one evening in late summer when all four of us headed for Birmingham City Centre on the train. I'd noticed there was more chat than usual; the mobile phones weren't stealing the kids' attention away like they normally did and it made for a much happier atmosphere.

The purpose of the visit was to see 'Van Gogh Alive'; a stunning interactive art exhibition that was touring the country. I'd suggested to Russ that it would do the boys good to be exposed to more art and culture (to my mind their lives were too IT-heavy and there wasn't enough focus on social interaction). Accommodating as ever, Russ agreed and sorted out the tickets.

There had been a lot of moaning initially from the lads. They'd got a game set up with friends, and asked did we have to go and see stupid pictures anyway? This was countered by a lot of encouragement from me, all the usual things adults would say, like 'There's a whole new world out there; art; films; food – it's important to try new things and have an open mind'.

I underpinned it all saying something like, "You don't want to end up like Kenny at the crem, now do you?"

I remember that had made everyone laugh. They still talked about the story of how Kenny was over-excited one day when I bumped into him. When asked why, he responded that he was "Having a week off to prepare for my week off innit?"

When I'd enquired what the dual weeks full of glittering promise consisted of, Kenny gleefully filled me in.

"Well it's gotta be right," he said, very seriously. "So the first week is to wash all me sweaters and have me hair cut; and the second week is to watch the football."

"So come on," I urged the boys, "Let's get cracking. Let's go and do some culture so your brains grow and you think bigger in life!"

In truth, I didn't know how the show would go down at all. I'm no expert on art or Vincent Van Gogh but the concept of it appealed to me. A high-tech, multi-sensory experience that told the incredibly sad story of an un-discovered genius. The man who produced so many of today's classics, but who back then, died in poverty, having only sold one painting in his lifetime. Bloody tragic probably sums it up.

For an hour or so we went on to lose ourselves in Van Gogh's world, spread around the entire interior of the Birmingham Hippodrome – a vast theatre that had been transformed for the occasion.

A total sensory journey, the show took us around the building, into the room set of his bedroom at Arles; the inspiration for one of his best-known paintings; and then on through a mirrored corridor of giant vibrant sunflowers.

From a combination of booklets, posters and of spoken words, we witnessed Vincent's story, from the early days of his apprenticeship, his romances and career. However, it was back on the main stage of the exhibition that his story truly came to life: (ironically, the same stage upon which I'd stood as a twenty year old in my first major talent show, and the one I'd performed on for the live TV show New Faces.)

As the music played, and Van Gogh's paintings scrolled down the wall, they were supported by his quotes. The words showed the genius and the disappointment of his life. His descent into madness, and the depth of his loneliness and despair, just prior to cutting off part of his own ear:

'I put my heart and my soul into my work and have lost my mind in the process.'

'I would rather die of passion than of boredom.'

And perhaps the saddest quote of all: 'I can't change the fact that my paintings don't sell. But the time will come when people recognise they are worth more than the value of the paints used in them.'

I joked ruefully with Russ about that last quote, harking back to all my writing stuffed in an office drawer. The un-produced musical; the rejected manuscripts; the songs and comedy show scripts. I remember wondering aloud if they'd ever be of interest to anyone.

I recall he'd smiled then saying, "Don't look back darling. You've got your new book to finish now; who knows? That may be the one. Just keep looking forward."

I think that was when he'd also asked if I still craved recognition. Some people who've been in entertainment can never let it go; partners always worry they'll disappear off at some stage, chasing the dream just one more time.

"Am I going to be enough for you long term?"

I remember being shocked. "Wow, of course! Where did that come from?"

"Nowhere," Russ said, looking visibly relieved. "I just had to ask – you looked so rueful then, as if something had passed you by. Or you were wrestling with a decision or something."

I told him not to be daft. That it was just a tad of melancholy. Dealing with death every week is beginning to drain me and I know I'm coming to the end of it all. There's really not much left in the tank, and if my creative pursuits continue to come to nothing, then what is there for me?

"Just look at these beautiful paintings Russ," I said. "Look at all the passion they contain. This man – this brilliant, gifted man – he lived for his work. He knew what he was here for. I just wonder sometimes, what my role is. I don't want to die unrecognised."

Russ shook his head. "Now who's the daft thing? You're more than recognised. You're appreciated, and loved. It doesn't have to be by 'the masses'. We can all make a lasting impact in our own little corner. Look at what trying to be famous did for poor Vincent." Again, he was putting things into perspective.

And then it was time to leave, to go for the boys' favourite bit of the evening – food!

"So lads, what do we want to eat tonight?"

Kyle replied that he didn't mind, but even as the words fell out of his mouth, he was drooling in front of a Mexican taco restaurant.

Aaron pulled his brother away, insisting he wanted a burger. But Russ reminded them this was a treat, and burgers were available any time at home. How about Japanese? he suggested.

I remember enjoying the push and pull of the family dynamic at that moment. Of being more than happy to be led along and try something new, so Japanese it was.

Minutes later we were ensconced in booths and presented with a menu I could barely read (no glasses) or understand.

Distracted, I remember watching the boys as they gently bickered and talked nonsense about video games, dogs and how much they hated school.

The food arrived. Kyle slurped his noodles loudly, explaining it was a sign of appreciation in the Japanese culture. His brother responded that it was just bad manners, and that he was gross. Russ rolled his eyes dramatically and told them both to behave.

The scene washed over and around me; the absurdity of the conversation and how endearing they actually were. And at that moment it struck me. That's how it is with kids. With kids that are relaxed and can be themselves.

I was getting there.

This was confirmed during the main course when Kyle looked up with a grin.

"Do you know it's my birthday next week?"

"Of course I do," I said. "And if it's okay with you, dad has invited me to go for dinner with you all?"

I waited with bated breath for the response. Just his second birthday with a different face at the table. It was a landmark moment.

Kyle met my eyes and smiled. "That's great then. We can all have pizza."

Barely a beat elapsed before he casually added; "Oh yes. And do you think you might like to live with us one day?"

Russ gulped quietly. His knee touched mine, just the gentlest of brushes. The atmosphere was electric.

"I think I'd like that very much Kyle."

Everyone grinned. The noodle slurping continued, barely interrupted.

Comfortable. As if we'd just had an easy conversation about the weather.

I remember feeling a sudden rush of happiness. A heady, deep happiness, at the realisation I no longer have to impress strangers with my efforts or seek approval from others. I am home.

And with that, the last quote from Van Gogh swam to the forefront of my mind:

'There is nothing more truly artistic than to love people.'

If that is so, then I perhaps I am about to create my masterpiece …

Printed in Great Britain
by Amazon

26633504R00096